The Art of Sanctions

CENTER ON GLOBAL ENERGY POLICY SERIES

CENTER ON GLOBAL ENERGY POLICY SERIES

JASON BORDOFF, SERIES EDITOR

Making smart energy policy choices requires approaching energy as a complex and multifaceted system in which decision-makers must balance economic, security, and environmental priorities. Too often, the public debate is dominated by platitudes and polarization. Columbia University's Center on Global Energy Policy at SIPA seeks to enrich the quality of energy dialogue and policy by providing an independent and nonpartisan platform for timely analysis and recommendations to address today's most pressing energy challenges. The Center on Global Energy Policy Series extends that mission by offering readers accessible, policy-relevant books that have as their foundation the academic rigor of one of the world's great research universities.

Robert McNally, *Crude Volatility: The History and the Future of Boom-Bust Oil Prices* (2017)

Daniel Raimi, *The Fracking Debate: The Risks, Benefits, and Uncertainties of the Shale Revolution* (2018)

The Art of Sanctions

A View from the Field

Richard Nephew

COLUMBIA UNIVERSITY PRESS

NEW YORK

Columbia University Press
Publishers Since 1893
New York Chichester, West Sussex
cup.columbia.edu
Copyright © 2018 Columbia University Press
Paperback edition, 2023

Library of Congress Cataloging-in-Publication Data
Names: Nephew, Richard, author.
Title: The art of sanctions : a view from the field / Richard Nephew.
Description: New York : Columbia University Press, [2018] |
Series: Center on Global Energy Policy series | Includes bibliographical
references and index.
Identifiers: LCCN 2017025803 | ISBN 9780231180269 (cloth) |
ISBN 9780231180276 (pbk.) | ISBN 9780231542555 (e-book)
Subjects: LCSH: Economic sanctions. | Economic sanctions—Iran—Case studies. |
Economic sanctions—Iraq—Case studies. | International economic
relations. | International relations.
Classification: LCC HF1413.5 .N47 2018 | DDC 327.1/17—dc23
LC record available at https://lccn.loc.gov/2017025803

Cover design: Fifth Letter
Printed and bound by CPI Group (UK) Ltd, Croydon, CR0 4YY

Contents

Contents

Preface

THIS IS A BOOK about the use of sanctions in foreign policy, written by a practitioner largely for practitioners and those operating in foreign policy more generally. It puts sanctions in the context of overall foreign policy strategy and uses terms that have been deliberately chosen for their visceral nature, such as *pain* and *tolerance*. It frames sanctions not in absolute terms of what works and what does not, but rather with respect to which critical questions must be answered and what information must be gathered prior to embarking on a sanctions campaign and how sanctions should be structured on the basis of those context-specific answers. Importantly, this book is intended to give those people whose careers and interest touch on the practical execution of foreign policy a mental framework for considering whether, when, and how to apply sanctions. It is designed to spell out the issues that sanctioners must confront. And it makes a case for a degree of humility in the design of sanctions, accepting that successful sanctions campaigns may be iterative, incremental activities of trial and error that are disconnected from the ivory tower of sanctions theory.

To that end, this book is not a rigorous, model-based examination of sanctions cases throughout history. There are books that offer exactly this kind of analysis, and I'd encourage those interested in such an analysis to dive in. One exemplary book on sanctions—now in its third edition—is Gary Hufbauer, Jeffrey Schott, and Kimberly Ann Elliot's *Economic Sanctions Reconsidered*. This book describes in terrific detail the nature of sanctions regimes stretching back through history and their overall impact in achieving the strategy that was pursued. It also offers clear lessons about the future conduct of sanctions and what combinations of tools may prove most effective in sanctions programs to come. Richard Pape's oft-cited article in *International Security*, "Why Economic Sanctions Don't Work," approaches the issue in a similar way. Similarly, his subsequent conversation with David Baldwin, also printed in *International Security*, is particularly useful in spelling out the application of sanctions pressure in the past and raising questions about measures of success. Likewise, other books address at some length the value of sanctions in economic statecraft, such as David Baldwin's seminal *Economic Statecraft* and Dan Drezner's *The Sanctions Paradox*. Robert Blackwill and Jen Harris's more recent *War by Other Means* and Juan Zarate's *Treasury's War* address these issues and reflect on some of the same cases presented here. These are just a few of the hundreds of books and articles written in the past few decades that seek to tackle the central question of "do sanctions work and how?"

Each of these works helps to inform the debate on sanctions, their effectiveness, and their place in modern statecraft. But what I hope to present in this book is an appraisal of more basic factors—how sanctions impose pain, how pain works, how pain translates into action on the part of the recipient, how resolve works, how it is communicated, and how it influences the outcome of a sanctions effort—in conjunction with the over-arching question of how sanctions ought to be configured in order to fit, complement, and support a broader national strategy to address a particular problem.

This book seeks to fill that niche, largely by focusing on the Iran case of recent memory.

My perspective is that of a policymaker whose career centered on the design and application of sanctions against Iran in response to its development of a nuclear program that the United States believed could—if not would—result in Iran's acquisition of nuclear weapons. I am biased in support of the contention that sanctions played a major part in changing Iran's approach to the negotiations around its nuclear program, and I defend the subsequent nuclear deal with Iran as an acceptable quid pro quo for sanctions removal. At the time of this writing, that nuclear deal still holds, though it may be subject to intensified strains as the Trump administration further solidifies its Iran policy and the Middle East continues along its turbulent course. I hope to shed some light on how sanctions policymakers think about these problems, how they work to implement strategies to confront them, where we have gone right and gone wrong, and what may come.

Despite the wealth of academic research on them, sanctions programs continue to be developed that fail to achieve their fundamental goals. Thus it is worth focusing again on basic questions: What are sanctions meant to do, and how do they relate to the basics of human interaction? The book's title gets to this idea. Though scientific examination of some elements of sanctions imposition is warranted, I believe sanctions design will likely remain an art form, requiring flexibility, adaptability, and intuition as much as rigorous consideration of mathematical abstractions.

At its heart, this book focuses on people and how they react to pressure. It offers suggestions about how to ensure that these reactions are consistent with the interests of the pressing party. It concentrates on the relationship that exists between a state's application of pain against another state via sanctions to achieve a defined objective and the readiness of sanctions targets to resist, tolerate, or overcome this pain and pursue their own agendas. It seeks to demonstrate that this relationship is critical for making any determination as to the effectiveness of sanctions as an implement of strategy. And it also highlights the importance of focusing on sanctions design, not just to evaluate how measures can be targeted but also to decide whether the application of sanctions will be at all useful, regardless of how craftily employed.

Acknowledgments

THIS BOOK TOOK A long time to come to fruition, starting as it did with late-night drives home from work at the National Security Council and State Department, and then continuing with sunny bike rides to and from Columbia University. It changed significantly across many drafts and was not without frustration, but I persevered in writing it largely because two people convinced me that it was worth the effort: Professor Bob Jervis, a legend in the field of international affairs, and my wife, Erin Nephew. The former stressed to me the importance of telling some of what I've learned . . . the latter reminded me that, though many have studied sanctions, all too few have worked on them and made them work in turn. I hope you find it constructive.

I want to thank Shirin Jamshidi and Joel Smith for their assistance in the researching of this book, as well as Colleen Stack, Peter Harrell, and Erin for their very helpful early review and comments on the text.

I also want to thank my editor, Bridget Flannery-McCoy, for her thoughtful work in making this an accessible and hopefully interesting product.

I would also like to thank the staff of the Center on Global Energy Policy, especially Jesse McCormick and Matt Robinson, for their assistance in getting the book from a vague idea to the typed page, and the director of the Center, Jason Bordoff, for sheltering me, yet another U.S. government expat, as I worked on it.

I want to thank my family for their loving support while I was engaged in both the writing of this book and the practice of sanctions that gave rise to it. My three children—Kiran, Amara, and Elijah—were born while I was about this business, and they sustained me as I spent countless days and nights away from home. My parents—Mike and Dorothy Nephew—and in-laws—Bob and Laura Engasser—pitched in to keep the ship afloat, while Erin steered. I treasure you all.

Last, this book is dedicated to the many people in the U.S. government and those of our partners with whom I worked for so many years on the challenge of Iran's nuclear program. On November 24, the day that the Joint Plan of Action (JPOA) was adopted, I was in a bus heading from the InterContinental Hotel in Geneva, Switzerland, to the UN building where the agreement would be formally announced. It was around 3:00 A.M. I had not slept properly in a long time, and the day, night, and early morning had been somewhat tense. My memory of what I said and to whom after agreement was reached is mostly fuzzy. But I can clearly remember an e-mail exchange with two colleagues of mine from the State Department, Kurt Kessler and Geoff Odlum. They offered congratulations for my having played a role in the back-channel talks that led to the JPOA. I told them that this victory was not mine, nor was it even that of the people gathered in Geneva. It was a team win, achieved over decades of work by intelligence officers, military service-people, civil servants, sanctioners, Congressional staff, and diplomats. All dedicated public servants, committed to one goal. I learned so much from you and benefited from our friendships and enmities, our successes and failures. This book is for all of you, and may it help to explain to the uninitiated how real professionals—you—go about their business.

And, sadly, this book is also dedicated to my many colleagues who remained in government when Donald Trump took office with campaign promises that suggested willingness—if not an outright desire—to dismantle the JCPOA and to replace it with something "better." We now look forward to seeing whether his administration, which entered office extremely confident in their ability to better the Obama team across the board, can deliver on this promise. History will not regard them kindly if they fail—or indeed my own efforts if they succeed. Yet I hope and pray for their success.

The Art of Sanctions

Introduction

AUTHORS OF WORKS ON sanctions are required by practice, if not yet by law, to begin their projects with a reaffirmation that sanctions have been in use since the ancient Greeks. This emphasis of the historical basis of the instrument is intended to demonstrate that, though sanctions may take different forms today, there is continuity in foreign policy thinking no matter how the cultural or political contexts have changed.

But referring to this historical continuity obscures a fundamental difference in how sanctions were viewed in the past, how they are viewed and used today, and how they achieve results.

Prior to the past hundred years, sanctions were typically an extension of a hostile relationship, often if not always involving military action either before or after sanctions were deployed. Though there are examples of sanctions regimes prior to the 1900s in which the tool was considered itself a sufficient threat or punishment to prevent conflict and achieve a diplomatic victory, it was not until the 1900s that sanctions began to be wielded with any frequency as an independent instrument of foreign policy. This evolution may have had as much to do with the increasingly total nature of warfare—starting with World War I—as it did with a desire on the part of statesmen to avoid the bloodshed that would otherwise come with their international intrigue. With war increasingly violent and destructive, robbing states of their economic power and people of their lives, strategists began to seek new ways of imposing their will on opponents. Economic power seemed a ripe avenue for many, particularly in a Cold War environment that—for all its peripheral violence—did not include the direct confrontation many expected and feared.

Examining the strategy of sanctions—how they work in changing a sanctioned state's actions—is critical now because, like it or not, sanctions have become a favorite instrument of U.S. foreign policy and have the potential of becoming a favorite of other major global powers. Russia—when faced with a need to respond to the Turkish downing of one of its fighter jets over an airspace violation in 2016—chose the application of economic sanctions over more militaristic options, despite the apparent bellicosity of its present administration. Russia is not alone. China has similarly taken aim at South Korea's decision to accept the basing of a Terminal High Altitude Area Defense (THAAD) system from the United States in response to North Korean ballistic missile testing by targeting tourism, trade, and South Korean luxury hotels.[1] Since 1960, dozens of countries have used economic sanctions to enforce their will in a variety of settings.[2]

Yet, even as sanctions took on a new role in the foreign policy tool kit, they often remain trapped in a conceptual vacuum in public discourse, without form or function to govern assessment of their appropriate role in a state's strategy. The contours of success and failure of the tool in individual circumstances have been well studied. There are countless works by serious scholars of international affairs that assess the effectiveness of sanctions or compare the utility of this tool against others. But there are far fewer works on how sanctions are designed by practitioners and combined with other tools to deliver a comprehensive strategy.

This book is largely about the U.S. sanctions effort against Iran from 1996 to 2015, which I (and others) judge to have been successful as part of a broader strategy of preventing Iran's acquisition of nuclear weapons. Parts of it are written anecdotally, owing to my direct, personal involvement in this project. But these are anecdotes grounded in the facts, figures, and theories of sanctions design that were part of the overall endeavor. Moreover, this book is no memoir. Rather than fixate on individual incidents or salacious details (of which there are few, but perhaps more than might be imagined), this book seeks to present the U.S. sanctions campaign in its proper context of national strategy as a means of illustrating how sanctions can be done properly (even if through examples of tactical failures and setbacks).

To do so, this book will examine the two main attributes of a sanctions strategy: a sanctioning state applying pain against a target and the target state's resolve to persist in whatever it did to prompt sanctions. Through this analysis, this book aims to help development of sanctions strategies that identify the intersection of escalating pain and diminishing resolve, at which a diplomatic negotiation can be most effective. Iran will be the primary example, but others will also be noted in their proper context.

At its heart, this book focuses on the relationship that exists between a state's application of pain against another state via sanctions to achieve a defined objective and the readiness of sanctions targets to resist, tolerate, or overcome this pain and pursue its own agenda. It seeks to demonstrate that this relationship is critical for making any determination as to the effectiveness of sanctions as an implement of strategy. And, as further chapters will reveal, it also focuses on the importance of sanctions design not just in how measures can be targeted but also in evaluating whether they should be used at all.

From these central attributes comes a simple framework for sanctioning states to follow in order for sanctions to perform their expected function. A state must

- identify objectives for the imposition of pain and define minimum necessary remedial steps that the target state must take for pain to be removed;
- understand as much as possible the nature of the target, including its vulnerabilities, interests, commitment to whatever it did to prompt sanctions, and readiness to absorb pain;
- develop a strategy to carefully, methodically, and efficiently increase pain on those areas that are vulnerabilities while avoiding those that are not;
- monitor the execution of the strategy and continuously recalibrate its initial assumptions of target state resolve, the efficacy of the pain applied in shattering that resolve, and how best to improve the strategy;
- present the target state with a clear statement of the conditions necessary for the removal of pain and an offer to pursue any negotiations necessary to conclude an arrangement that removes the pain while satisfying the sanctioning state's requirements; and
- accept the possibility that, notwithstanding a carefully crafted strategy, the sanctioning state may fail because of inherent inefficiencies in the strategy, a misunderstanding of the target, or an exogenous boost in the target's resolve and capacity to resist. Either way, a state must be prepared either to acknowledge its failure and change its course or accept the risk that continuing with its present course could create worse outcomes in the long run.

To the last point, I take the perspective that sanctions do not fail or succeed. Rather, sanctions are either helpful to achieving the desired end result of a sanctioning state or not. A state (and a state's strategy) can be said to have succeeded or failed, including in the state's employ of sanctions as a tool to achieve its national strategy. But it is ridiculous to say that "sanctions" either succeed or fail independent of whether the strategy through which they were being employed succeeded or failed, just as it would be ridiculous to argue that military force does not "work" on the basis of one failed campaign or war. Plainly put, tools can only perform well when they are employed with a proper strategy; one can't blame the saw if it fails to perform the work of a screwdriver.

The case of Iran is instructive here. Simply by reading the newspapers in 2012, one could easily get the impression that sanctions were failing for a long time or that their failure was inevitable given the pace of Iranian technical achievement. And, after the initial nuclear deal was reached in 2013 (and consolidated in a comprehensive one in 2015), one could argue in contrast that sanctions were inevitably going to create the kind of condition in which a deal with Iran could be struck, success having been guaranteed the moment sanctions begun to bite. Both lines of argument are wrong. They take too linear an approach to sanctions application and too restrictive a mindset to their value. Sanctions worked in achieving a deal with Iran in 2013 because of the combined action of many moving parts of strategy (and perhaps a good measure of propitious timing and luck). They were a necessary but not sufficient condition for success. And in the execution of our sanctions-equipped strategy, the many deficiencies of the tool were exposed, from which we can learn much.

Before further developing this framework, I must define some of our terms and discuss their intellectual context, limits, and uses.

1

Defining Terms

MOST PEOPLE YOU MEET on the street can offer a workable definition of sanctions. They can identify the elements of sanctions—for example, prohibiting trade in particular items or in total—or they can describe the desired economic result, such as "preventing a country from engaging in normal business activity." But at some point, most definitions will mix the concept of penalties and consequences with the overarching system of rules and obligations that interfere with normal economic activity.

This conflation adds to the confusion about what "sanctions" constitute and how to ascertain their effectiveness. Let's take a concrete example: the United States has an extensive set of "sanctions" against Iran, even after the January 2016 implementation of the Joint Comprehensive Plan of Action (JCPOA). But the United States also imposes "sanctions" on individual actors identified as having violated "sanctions." And the United States imposes "sanctions" on individual actors who help others engaging in "sanctionable" conduct, which is itself a violation of "sanctions."

Another example shines a spotlight on the problems created by this semantic confusion: if "sanctions" refers both to an individual fine of several thousand dollars and an institutionalized set of rules and obligations governing trade between two major economies, then it is plainly more difficult to ascertain subsequently whether "sanctions" worked in a particular situation. "Sanctions" may have worked quite well in harming the business and reputation of the firm fined several thousand dollars, while "sanctions" also failed miserably in impeding the effort of a sanctioned country to support terrorism. To borrow a military allusion, this terminological problem is the equivalent of confusing the effectiveness of an army division with the overall progress of a war. The division may be successful while its comrades fail or vice versa, but the distinction certainly matters, in real life and in analysis.

To develop a strategy of sanctions, we must therefore understand what is meant in all uses of the word. Starting with the highest level of abstraction, *sanctions* are defined in this book as the constellation of laws, authorities, and obligations laid out in a piece of legislation, government decree, UN resolution, or similar document that restrict or prohibit what is normally permissible conduct and against which performance will be assessed and compliance judged. A synonym for *sanctions* in this usage is *sanctions regime*. In this framework, the "imposition of sanctions" should be read as creating a set of systemic, overarching rules of behavior. Violations of sanctions are therefore also to be read as contravening the overall sanctions regime by breaking the specific rules and terms.

Notably, these rules can cover all sorts of activity, not just economic activity. For instance, the UN Security Council (UNSC) has often used the imposition of travel bans as a way of applying pressure against individuals and their governments. These bans are hardly of economic value (at least in most instances), but they are applied nonetheless as a way of creating new restrictions governing the target. Likewise, such sanctions can also be framed around the denial of particular goods—such as those needed for the Iranian or North Korean missile programs—where the overall economic impact may be slight, but the strategic value is significant. For this reason, I modify the use of the term *sanctions* when appropriate to characterize the scope of the measures, whether the sanctions are economic, technological, or personal. Likewise, I will avoid using the term *sanctions* to define the direct imposition of penalties or consequences for a violation of the overall regime, preferring instead to describe them as penalties or consequences.

Why Impose Sanctions?

Sanctions are intended to create hardship—or to be blunt, "pain"—that is sufficiently onerous that the sanctions target changes its behavior.

Using *pain* as the specific word for the objective may seem provocative, loaded as it is with imagery of torture and abuse. Yet, *pain* is a useful term precisely because it is evocative; as a common human experience, people can instinctively appreciate what sanctions incur as well as the desire to avoid the resulting "pain." For this reason, I am not the first to use *pain* in this context.

Pain as a term underscores both the purpose of sanctions and their inherent limitations. Pain causes discomfort that most people seek to avoid, but it can also be managed, tolerated, and—over time—potentially adapted to, even to the profit of its recipient. Of course, the physical dimension of pain is less pronounced in sanctions, certainly as they have been practiced over the past decade with an increased emphasis on avoiding the curtailment of humanitarian trade, even with heavily sanctioned jurisdictions. In fact, the type of pain and its severity may be modulated, but the intention of sanctions is always to make the new status quo uncomfortable and unpleasant for the target. Sanctioned persons are expected to find the discomfort sufficiently onerous that they'll do something different. In this way, sanctions are a form of violence.

Pain avoidance is a significant impulse for the individual and, scaled up, for societies. Translating this basic impulse into a subject for international affairs analysis entered its heyday with the bevy of nuclear strategy manuals published in the 1950s. One of the foremost theorists of nuclear deterrence, the late Thomas Schelling, began his seminal work *Arms and Influence* with the observation that "the power to hurt—the sheer unacquisitive, unproductive power to destroy things that somebody treasures, to inflict pain and grief—is a kind of bargaining power, not easy to use but used often."[1] He goes on to note that "hurting, unlike forcible seizure or self defense, is not unconcerned with the interest of others. It is measured in the suffering it can cause and the victims' motivation to avoid it."[2]

Schelling was speaking primarily of the use of military force as a motivating factor, as opposed to sanctions, but the concepts are essentially the same. So too are concepts of resolve, which Schelling dubs at one point "endurance."[3] They relate to a country's ability to absorb pain and still maintain its ability to function. In many cases, this is described in military terms, but as with pain, this ability need not be: the ability of an economy to continue functioning despite losing a major part of its productive capacity is analogous to an army continuing to fight despite losing a division.

Because of the different practical effects of sanctions and military force, however, policymakers treat these two tools far differently. Military conflict creates casualties and damage for each side, and the results are visible for all to see. The impact of sanctions can be less visible and may seem less destructive, certainly on a visceral level. This no doubt explains part of the attractiveness of sanctions as a tool of force: it is preferable by far for a politician or national security official to accept and defend the loss of 1/4 percent of GDP than it is to accept and defend the loss of a thousand military servicepeople and civilians. But on a strategic level, the imposition of pain via sanctions is intended to register the same impulses in an adversary as those imposed via military force: to face a choice between capitulation and resistance, between the comparatively easy path of compromise and the sterner path of confrontation. And just because the damage wrought by sanctions may be less visible (at least, with some sanctions regimes), it need not be less destructive, particularly for economically vulnerable populations that may be affected.

Big changes in policy—such as giving up a claim to a territory—may require more pain than smaller changes in policy, such as stopping arms trade with an insurgent group. But sanctioning countries may not be totally aware of the scope of the measures they intend to pursue, miscalculating at times as the resolve of their adversary and whether the pain inflicted is having the intended effect. Deciding how to impose pain that is effective (and, hopefully, efficient) is an issue for intelligence analysts and sanctions experts. But at the root of their efforts is the desire to inflict some measure of pain in order to change policy, as well as an inclination to match pain levels with the desired outcome.

Unfortunately, those entities imposing sanctions often downplay this concept of imposing pain, at least with respect to anyone other than the desired target. The reasons are myriad but, in my experience, were largely to avoid ownership of humanitarian consequences. As we shall see in later chapters, the emphasis in the United States on the targeted aspect of sanctions after a period of excess in Iraq in the 1990s is a manifestation of this desire. Sanctions literature has, possibly inadvertently, helped contribute to a perception of relative bloodlessness of sanctions after Iraq, contrasting new "smart" sanctions with presumably old "dumb" sanctions.

Certainly, it is easier to defend the negative impacts on the sanctioned jurisdiction by arguing, with some plausibility, that these effects are not solely to do with sanctions or—even better—that only the desired negative effects stem from sanctions. Such a framework allows a sanctioner to avoid claiming responsibility for humanitarian problems stemming from sanctions, while making the connections clear when claiming credit for sanctions' benefits. The U.S. government has maintained for years that, since its sanctions policies target the Iranian government and bad actors, its responsibility is minimal for any humanitarian problems resulting from economic pressure applied. But such claims do tend to ring hollow when considered simply and without the artifice of policy analysis. After all, if you intentionally reduce a country's ability to earn foreign currency through exports, then you will almost by definition create at least some pressure on imports, including of food and medicine. True, a sanctioner can always point out that it is the responsibility of the sanctioned country to manage its imports and even to avoid the entire confrontation. But this does not mean that sanctions were not painful, including at the street level, or that the sanctioner is innocent of having created any resulting crisis. Moreover, the irony of all this is that sanctions are ultimately intended to cause pain and change policy: denying some of that pain may make for better public relations for a sanctions program, but it also undermines the contention that sanctions work and may even interfere with their effectiveness on a practical level if a sanctioner adjusts the regime to address a humanitarian problem and, in doing so, reduces the very pain the sanctions are intended to create.

This leads to a fundamental set of questions: how do you tailor sanctions to achieve their objectives with the minimum *necessary* pain on the sanctioned target? How do you undermine willingness to endure this pain when the target has already been informed that the desired effect is bounded? How do you communicate readiness to exceed the amount of pain established to break down this resolve? And is there an optimal point at which pressure has been brought to bear sufficient to achieve your desired result, without having to go farther?

What Is Resolve?

The answer to these questions lies in an understanding of the impact of sanctions and their pain on the targeted state, particularly the response of the sanctions target and how it accepts, resists, or works around the pain being imposed by the sanctioner.

I will use the term *resolve* to capture the overarching concept of a target's response to sanctions and readiness to continue with its objectionable activity. In this way, *resolve* is perhaps defined best as the simple, psychological determination of the sanctioned state to deny victory to the sanctioning party and to persevere with its chosen path. This determination can come from many sources—including a desire to avoid whatever disruptions may come from deviating from present policy—but the key factor is the degree to which the target believes that its present approach is better than the sanctioner's identified alternative despite obvious pressure to change course. And, in fact, sanctions are themselves intended to undermine this psychological determination, both by undermining its physical basis (for example, if a target fears the economic damage of acceding to the sanctioner's desired approach, then a sanctioner escalates the economic damage of *not* acceding to the sanctioner's desired approach) and the target's willingness to absorb it (for example, by making acquiescence to the sanctioner's demand seem inevitable).

States can undertake a variety of strategies to manage or combat inflicted pain. They can accept the pain, making do with the impact of it and carrying on regardless. They can reject the pain, seeking to evade the impact of sanctions through smuggling or erection of power blocs opposed to the imposition of sanctions in the first place. And, in a hybrid approach, states can adapt to the pain, absorbing it where necessary and taking advantage of its consequences where possible to identify new areas of economic activity or political cooperation.

As this is a book on the strategy of sanctions rather than sanctions rejection, the focus of the following analysis is on how sanctioners experience and respond to demonstrations of resolve, seeking to overcome them and manage their own problems with commitment, expressed most often as "sanctions fatigue." But, as these pages will show, without a solid understanding of how states struggle against the imposition of pain, sanctioners are impaired in their ability to define and implement effective sanctions. As Ned Lebow pointed out in the conclusion of *Psychology and Deterrence,*

> policy makers who risk or actually start wars pay more attention to their own strategic and domestic political interests than they do to the interests and military capabilities of their adversaries . . . [T]hey may discount an adversary's resolve even when the state in question has gone to considerable lengths to demonstrate that resolve and to develop the military capabilities needed to defend its commitment.[4]

It does not take much imagination to substitute Lebow's military terms with economic terms in order to see that a close parallel can be made with those who impose economic force or any of the other forms of pressure that sanctions can bring. As with the use of military threats, the encapsulating strategy in which sanctions are imposed cannot hope to succeed if there is a misunderstanding of the natural and adopted resolve levels of sanctions targets.

For such an important element of sanctions-related theory, resolve is neither readily understood nor accommodated in most sanctions programs. Instead, resolve can be sometimes treated as a routine commodity, with equal weight given to different sanctions tools across different contexts. It may often be assumed, for instance, that depriving any country of gasoline will lead to not only economic but also social crises, perhaps because—from an American-centric view—taking away the ability to use automobiles at will is a violation of a God-given right. But for a country where the primary personal means of public transportation is electrically driven trains, the impact of a gasoline ban may be far less severe.

Discussions of sanctions imposition sometimes assume that an adversary will experience the same pain as the sanctioner would perceive should the tables be turned. But such an approach misses the cultural, economic, political, and broader social dynamics that might change the impact of sanctions. These factors have real salience. They can represent the difference between sanctions achieving their intended objective or failing. And, in some cases, failure to consider national circumstances carefully could even lead to sanctions being imposed that create greater resolve in the targeted state than otherwise could be expected or—for that matter—sanctions being imposed that are perversely welcomed by their target for domestic political or economic reasons, or even to improve their position internationally.

This last reflection lends emphasis to a central problem of sanctions as a foreign-policy tool: a lack of understanding as to whether the pain imposed by the sanctioner has the intended impact on the target state, as well as how the targeted state will choose to respond. This problem plagues many different elements of foreign policy decision making, but perhaps with no worse a negative impact than in the realm of sanctions, where the psychological battle between opponents is the most pronounced. While military force also requires consideration of psychological resilience and will, ultimately it can render an opponent physically incapacitated even should the opponent's resolve never falter. This is far harder to achieve via sanctions, particularly in an increasingly globalized world with goods available from a variety of providers and with video cameras, Twitter, and Instagram available on every phone.

With sanctions, states are almost always placed in a game of chicken, each daring the other to swerve and with damage resulting to both parties from the conflict. For the sanctioned state, the impacts are part and parcel of the sanctions themselves. For the sanctioning state, the impact is often subtler but could involve economic harm, diplomatic disruption (as the sanctions regime demands senior-level focus to maintain it and constant engagement with sanctions partners to keep them on-side), and the creation of an escalating commitment trap, in which a state feels it cannot walk away from the sanctions regime without achieving victory, lest it lose credibility in any future crisis. A crucial element in the imposition of sanctions is therefore the understanding of relative levels of national resolve being brought to the table and what kind of steps can be taken to reduce them.

In the end, I conclude that knowledge of one's opponent, their tolerances, and their vulnerabilities is the most important predictor of a sanctions-focused strategy's chances for success. All too often, sanctions advocates conflate their own desire to demonstrate their commitment to sanctions with considerations of resolve in their targets. Advocates assume that to fail to act is to show weakness and that the tougher the action, the better. In such a simplistic, naïve, and misguided fashion, sanctions advocates fall into a trap that military strategists throughout history and across cultures have drilled into their acolytes: failing to understand their opponent fully before committing to the field. In fact, for sanctions to work, one must actually know one's enemy better than the enemy knows itself.

The United States has both succeeded and failed at this task in the past. But to understand how current sanctions practitioners work through this problem, we must first examine a critical failure: that of the sanctions regime against Iraq from 1990 to 2003.

2

Iraq

THE INTERNATIONAL COMMUNITY IMPOSED sanctions regimes against Iraq in the 1990s and against Iran in the 2000s that could not be more different in structure, legal basis, and direct consequences. In fact, while the sanctions against Iran have been praised as being exceptionally targeted and effective (at least in some quarters), most descriptions of the sanctions against Iraq would characterize them as the unenlightened forebear of Iran sanctions, serving as an object lesson of "how not to do it" for future sanctioners to study.

Iraq's Invasion of Kuwait and Own Invasion in Turn

On August 2, 1990, Iraqi tanks stormed across their southern border into Kuwait. The Iraqi invasion took place following months of increased tensions between the two countries over oil-field drilling and extraction, Iraqi financial problems created by the Iran-Iraq War (1980–1988), and poor signaling by the Iraqis, other Gulf

Arab states, the United States, and the rest of the international community about the possibility of an invasion and how it would be treated.[1] Saddam Hussein, in particular, seemed to believe that the rest of the world would accept an invasion of Kuwait, and, even if they did not, he believed he had the military capability to prevent significant retaliation. Iraq's invasion was a flagrant violation of the UN Charter and moreover a rejection of the very principles upon which the United Nations was founded: respect for national sovereignty and the peaceful resolution of disputes. Hussein's actions set a context for international response that was highly persuasive on its face. Every state around the world has borders. Many states have borders that are unresolved, and some even have borders with states that possess military forces that are quantum leaps above their own domestic capabilities. The invasion of Iraq was not just therefore an affront to the international order; it presaged a potential security calamity for the rest of the Middle East and those around the world who feared what their own local bullies might do next. The timing of Iraq's invasion was also notable, coming as the Cold War was itself ending and as leaders around the world were looking for a new paradigm for managing international security and stability.

The UN Security Council (UNSC) responded to the invasion by slapping sanctions on Iraq within four days. UNSC resolution (UNSCR) 661 imposed, among other things, an arms embargo against Iraq, and it warned of future measures. UNSCR 661 was itself both an expression of commitment by the international community against Iraqi occupation and a set of consequences. It was swiftly supplemented during the following five months by other sanctions resolutions, six in all, forming in aggregate a comprehensive sanctions regime against Iraq. Ultimately, these sanctions did not convince Saddam Hussein to withdraw from Kuwait. Instead, an international coalition led by the United States initiated a military operation in January 1991 to expel Iraq. But sanctions remained in place even after the conclusion of active hostilities as a way of managing Saddam's militant impulses and providing reassurance to his neighbors. From 1990 forward, sanctions interrupted normal trade and business until after the U.S.-led "coalition of the willing" invasion of Iraq in 2003.

Key elements of the sanctions regime included prohibitions on

- the import of all products and commodities originating in Iraq;
- any activities by UN member nations in Iraq that would promote the export of products originating in Iraq;
- the availability of funds or other financial or economic resources to Iraq, or to any commercial, industrial, or public utility operating within it, except for medical or humanitarian purposes; and
- the sale of weapons or other military equipment, as well as other goods, to Iraq.

A consequence of this severe sanctions regime was the near-complete collapse of all forms of trade with Iraq, made worse by Iraq's inability (or, given Saddam Hussein's predilection for palace building, refusal) to ensure the availability of hard currency for humanitarian goods. The international community attempted to lessen the humanitarian impact of sanctions against Iraq during this period. For example, in 1995, the UNSC authorized the sale of limited amounts of Iraqi oil in order to provide an economic lifeline for the Iraqi population. The "Oil for Food" program, as it was subsequently dubbed, was found to be riddled with corruption, but it had a positive impact on the supply of humanitarian goods to the Iraqi population. This aside, the sanctions regime against Iraq was intense, robust, and effective in that Iraq was denied any possibility of being able to rearm itself, whether by conventional or unconventional means. In this fashion, a key aim of the sanctions regime was achieved.

However, there was no common understanding of what would be required in order to achieve complete satisfaction of the international community's concerns with Iraq. Certainly, the text of UNSCR 687 (1991) outlined what Iraq must do, particularly with respect to its obligations to disclose and dismantle any programs for producing weapons of mass destruction and ballistic missiles. Other steps included accepting the international boundary between Iraq and Kuwait as it was prior to the invasion of Kuwait, permitting inspection of any sites in Iraq associated with weapons of mass destruction (WMD) programs and missiles, repayment of Iraqi sovereign debts, Iraqi renouncement of terrorism, and Iraqi acceptance of international humanitarian missions, such as that of the Red Cross, into its territory. But when Iraq failed to cooperate fully and transparently in addressing lingering concerns with its WMD programs, the United States, United Kingdom, and other states understood Iraq's refusal to be both a violation of Iraq's UNSC obligations as well as confirmation that the Iraqis intended to pursue weapons of mass destruction.

This misconception proved disastrous, in that it led directly to the invasion of Iraq by the United States and its partners in the "coalition of the willing" in March 2003, even though—as we learned afterwards—Iraq had no WMD or easy means to reconstitute WMD programs. The invasion itself marked the effective end of the use of sanctions as a point of leverage over Iraq. But what is of particular interest is the logic behind Saddam Hussein's provocation of US and UK moves to war prior to 2002. Hussein certainly had it within his power to cooperate with international demands to provide access to any facility in the country. On the other hand, Hussein felt that Iraqi national sovereignty and his dignity as its executive were undermined by capitulation to Western demands. That Hussein was a megalomaniac who murdered thousands of his people does not diminish his own sense of self, his nationalism, and the impact that these factors had on his decision making.

In fact, Saddam Hussein's control over the country may have made things worse from the standpoint of resolving the situation without the United States and its partners resorting to violence. In other countries, democratic pressure or the interests of other groups might have influenced the leader's decision making to ensure he accepted an accommodation that removed the need for—and credibility of—an invasion. In fact, one could look at Iraq's readiness to accept a renewed inspection effort in 2002 as precisely this kind of dynamic. However, the United States maintained at the end of 2002 and 2003 that Iraq's declarations to international inspectors contained gaps, particularly about its efforts to develop WMD in the past, that amounted to material violations of its continuing disarmament and nonproliferation obligations. The UN's chief inspector, Hans Blix, noted in his statement to the UNSC on March 7, 2003, the conundrum facing the international community:

> It is obvious that while the numerous initiatives which are now taken by the Iraqi side with a view to resolving some longstanding, open disarmament issues can be seen as active or even proactive, these initiatives three to four months into the new resolution cannot be said to constitute immediate cooperation. Nor do they necessarily cover all areas of relevance. They are, nevertheless, welcome. And UNMOVIC [UN Monitoring, Verification and Inspection Commission] is responding to them in the hope of solving presently unresolved disarmament issues.[2]

In other words, Iraq had not met its obligation to provide the level of cooperation sought by the United States and its partners, even though it did provide far more cooperation and access than before Blix's renewed mission in 2002. The United States and its partners did not accept such a mixed grade as indicative of a more positive interpretation of Hussein's behavior and intention. Rather, the point of emphasis for the United States was on the absence of immediate, comprehensive cooperation, which suggested a desire to evade international scrutiny in order to protect illicit weapons programs. But the more interesting revelation from this story is that Hussein had every opportunity to go farther in his country's admissions if he wanted to. He had no illicit weapons program to be discovered. Had he accepted the transparency and monitoring demanded of him, he might have disarmed the United States and its partners, preserving his regime. But he chose not to, notwithstanding the potential consequences. Why?

Many have written on this subject, positing a range of explanations. The CIA's report on Iraq's WMD program after the 2003 invasion cites four main reasons:

- the desire to avoid looking weak, especially with respect to regional adversaries like Iran and Israel
- the desire to preserve an image of a great and powerful Iraq on the international stage
- Hussein's fear of his subordinates building a coalition and rising against him; and
- the perception of Iraq's nuclear program as a logical result of technological advancement and an opportunity to highlight Iraq's technological capabilities.[3]

Put a different way, as perverse as it may appear, Hussein's ordering of Iraqi national interests put the imminent loss of territorial integrity through Western invasion *below* his desire to avoid being perceived as weak at home or abroad. He was prepared to court the possibility of invasion, notwithstanding all indications of readiness to act on the part of the United States and its partners, because either he doubted the resolve of the coalition or feared the consequences of cooperation. This was something that U.S. policymakers fully understood only after the invasion.

Drawing Lessons for Sanctions

Altogether, the Iraq case has interesting implications for our study of sanctions pressure. Implicitly, this means that though a combination of sanctions and potential military pressure were powerful insofar as their consequences for the Iraqi population, its future WMD programs, and its conventional military strength were concerned, Hussein did not believe these pressures were sufficient to force his full cooperation with international inspectors. Beyond suggesting that sanctions pressure might have had little continued value in seeking this kind of cooperation from Iraq (buttressing the U.S. administration's argument at the time that continued sanctions would not solve the underlying problem), this assessment also supports a different contention: that no matter how forcefully sanctions had been used against Iraq, they had a maximum value insofar as diminishing Iraqi resolve is concerned. The Iraqis—or, at least, Saddam Hussein—established an incredibly high bar for what would be required for him to feel compelled to cooperate fully and transparently with UN WMD inspectors. No matter how much sanctions pressure could be mounted, it would not shift his mindset.

This episode also underscores an important point about the study of sanctions, or rather a study of how to make them work properly: how difficult it is to assess in advance the degree to which pain will be tolerated, what types of pain are most meaningful for individual targets, and the resolve of a regime.

The Iraqi economy had collapsed for all intents and purposes in the 1990s (though, as O'Sullivan notes, it was in poor shape prior to the invasion of Kuwait following the eight-year-long Iran-Iraq War and in much worse condition after U.S. airstrikes during the First Gulf War).[4] Some economic activity remained, and people had jobs, sources of income, and ways to spend what they earned. But the downturn for Iraq after the beginning of sanctions was stark, as sanctions reduced Iraq's economic capacity and ability to rebuild after the two wars:

- Real earnings fell by 90 percent during the first year, and then by 40 percent between 1991 and 1996.
- Industrial production decreased by 80 percent.
- By 1996, public sector workers commonly earned $3 to $5 per month compared to their pre-sanctions salaries of $150 to $200 per month.[5]

Saddam Hussein proved remarkably resistant to the pressure of these sanctions. Certainly, he himself was not suffering. He could not exert himself internationally, but he built nine luxurious palaces worth $2 billion during the 1990s.[6] Moreover, he resisted opportunities to address his people's concerns, even short of offering the kind of full cooperation with the United Nations that might have led to sanctions being eased or terminated. For example, the United Nations established the legal underpinnings of the "Oil for Food" program in 1991, but Hussein declined opportunities to activate the program until 1996, when the international community essentially foisted it upon him.[7] Even though now the program is much maligned because of the corruption that it enabled in Iraq and at the United Nations, the program itself had a simple, humanitarian justification that Hussein spurned for years. And, of course, he engaged in countless atrocities at home that demonstrated his lack of interest in the well-being of his population.

Hussein's defiance suggested to U.S. and international observers that he was extremely dedicated to preserving his WMD ambitions. His ability to evade to a significant degree the sanctions imposed on him suggested that sanctions were ineffective in managing Iraq as a whole. But perhaps instead he was simply committed to keeping everyone in the international community guessing, as well as holding firm on his protection of Iraqi national rights. This speaks to an important and complicated dimension for measuring resolve: the level of significance to give to particular points of evidence and what each individual piece means for a country's defense of the particular interests in question. Though at the time Hussein was suspected of being resolute in defense of Iraq's nascent WMD capabilities, it appears now that Hussein was instead resolute in defense of Iraqi sovereignty while not possessing any significant WMD capabilities. This is meaningful not only for future scenarios of nonproliferation and arms control failures but also for evaluation of how a country reacts to pressure. Having been successful in preventing Iraqi rearmament and in dismantling Iraq's WMD infrastructure, sanctions achieved their purpose and outlived their usefulness. But failure to understand that success had been achieved with respect to the narrow set of issues that prompted the imposition of sanctions—and to grasp that the remaining issues were beyond the reach of sanctions—led to perceptions in the United States and beyond that the sanctions regime itself had failed.

In the end, it was not sanctions that failed, but rather the failure of Iraqi, U.S., and other U.S. partners' policymakers to understand properly the considerable stakes of resolve, credibility, and prestige that were in conflict. The initial problem had been solved, but the solution was not recognized.

From our perspective, several deficiencies can be seen in the handling of Iraq through this period. First and foremost, there were confused objectives for the imposition of pain. But worse, there was ambiguity about whether those objectives had been met because some parties—the United States and the United Kingdom, in particular—held a higher bar than others for Iraqi performance. This confusion contributed to sanctions fatigue. It also meant that, when the United States and the United Kingdom presented a case to the international community about the need for war, the support for action simply was not there. Second, there was little understanding about the commitment of Saddam Hussein to his rejectionist course, even as there was significant understanding of

Iraq's economy and its vulnerabilities. This, in the end, only served to strengthen the conviction among those in the United States and elsewhere that Iraq was pursuing nuclear and other weapons of mass destruction, for only in this cause would such deprivation be justified. In this, policymakers and intelligence analysts implicitly applied their own sense of standards for sanctioned-state resolve and thereby misdiagnosed both the problems in Iraq and the solutions. Third, because the sanctions had been maximized within the first six months, there was no opportunity for an incremental and efficient increase in pain over a longer span of time. Rather, the maximum allotment of sanctions pain was assigned in 1991, meaning that there was no further ratcheting up available and therefore little means of signaling a sanctioning state's willingness to go farther. The absence of further steps to take in the realm of sanctions may have contributed to a sense of fatalism in Iraq that was ultimately counterproductive. And last, there was no recourse for resolution of the problems surrounding Iraqi compliance with its UNSC obligations other than military action. This lack of resolution is not, itself, a failure of the sanctions regime but rather of the underlying policy, which did not provide for serious consideration of the possibility of success in the comprehensive embargo and—consequently—did not budget for off-ramps short of complete Iraqi capitulation. Arguably, even with complete capitulation, the United States and its partners might still have made a case that Iraq's longstanding perfidy and Saddam Hussein's own personal crimes undermined the value of any concessions Iraq might make.

Either consciously or not, these were all mistakes that the United States sought to avoid when imposing sanctions on Iran.

3

Taking on Iran

AMERICAN OFFICIALS LEARNED MUCH from the experience with Iraq. Some of this learning shaped the response to concerns with Iran's nuclear program, which existed throughout the 1990s but exploded into the public consciousness in August 2002 with revelations that Iran had been constructing two secret nuclear facilities. These revelations prompted an international investigation, led by the International Atomic Energy Agency (IAEA), and—ultimately—both the imposition of sweeping sanctions against Iran and the nuclear deal that began the process of removing those same sanctions in 2015.

Iranian Nuclear History, in Brief

Contrary perhaps to some expectations, Iran's nuclear program did not begin under its present government, the post-revolution Islamic Republic. Rather, it began under the previous government of the Shah of Iran, who ruled Iran from 1941 to 1979 (with a brief interruption in 1953). He began the Iranian nuclear program as both a potential energy source and as a way of advancing the country's overall scientific capacity. The nuclear program was the subject of considerable internal investment of treasure and talent. The West helped. In 1967, Iran acquired a research reactor from the United States (along with highly enriched uranium fuel). Hundreds of Iranian students were dispatched to a variety of Western institutions to learn what they could of nuclear physics and related disciplines after the creation of the Atomic Energy Organization of Iran in 1974.[1] The Shah's Iran spent considerably to develop a rudimentary nuclear infrastructure and to lay the groundwork for more, with the budget of the Atomic Energy Organization reaching $1 billion in 1976 alone.[2] The twin nuclear power reactors planned for Bushehr were to be the crowning achievement of the Shah's nuclear program, but by far not its terminus: Iran was to have at least 23,000 megawatts (electric) by 1994.[3] And hidden under the surface but a paramount concern for the United States (at least for a time), the Shah also appears to have been interested in applying his country's burgeoning nuclear expertise toward nuclear weapons. He sought a variety of technologies that have a place in civil nuclear energy production, but which are also essential for the production of nuclear material for weapons. These technologies—which constitute what is known as the nuclear "fuel cycle"—include spent fuel reprocessing (that can support plutonium-based weapons) and uranium enrichment (that can support uranium-based weapons). It was the Shah's interest in developing spent fuel reprocessing in particular that prompted concern in the United States as to his overall ambitions.

It appears today that the Shah was motivated to consider nuclear power as a means of delivering reliable energy supply, providing insurance for a future in which Iranian oil and gas might not be available for electricity production, and spurring further technical innovation; he sought a nuclear weapons option as a way of managing regional security issues, deterring Western or Soviet interference, and demonstrating the sophistication and majesty of the Iranian people. In this, there is a corollary to the Shah's massive acquisition of conventional weapons with the oil boom of the early 1970s, which some have speculated stemmed both from his regional ambitions and a fundamental sense of regime insecurity.[4]

After the Iranian revolution in 1979, there was less interest in a nuclear program, in part due to the expense.[5] As much as the Iranian revolution took a religious tone over time, it began as an economic protest against extravagant spending by the Shah while economic inequality wracked the broader population. The nuclear program was lumped into this same category by the revolutionary government. But by the mid-1980s, the Iranian nuclear program was once more funded and pursuing a variety of technology lines. Some of these activities were legitimately associated with civil applications, such as nuclear power or the production of medical isotopes for the treatment of disease. Iran also sought technical cooperation from a variety of sources, including the IAEA and a number of individual countries, in order to expand its knowledge base and capabilities.

However, we also now know that, beginning in the late 1980s and continuing through the early 2000s, Iran once more pursued technologies that could contribute directly to the development and acquisition of nuclear weapons. Some of this covert work Iran did on its own, but much of it was supported through technology purchases and technical assistance from the father of Pakistan's nuclear weapons program, Abdul Qadeer Khan.[6] Khan had started Pakistan's nuclear weapons program through the illicit acquisition of technology from his former employer, URENCO, and, in time, he used his connections with companies around the world to create what became known as the "A. Q. Khan" proliferation network. While active, this network transferred sensitive nuclear technology and designs to Libya, in addition to Iran. It may have also supported nuclear weapons research in Iraq, Syria, and North Korea (although this has yet to be proven).[7]

Iran's purchases centered on the production of material usable for nuclear weapons through the use of uranium centrifuges, and the country procured two designs and several prototype centrifuges from Khan to advance its program. Combined with Iran's work to develop a nuclear warhead—possibly through the application of still further information bought from Khan—Iran's nuclear program was bifurcated into a declared program and an undeclared one. The declared program operated on the surface, with facilities made known to the IAEA and—through the IAEA—the rest of the world in accordance with Iran's obligations under the Treaty on the Nonproliferation of Nuclear Weapons (NPT) and its Comprehensive Safeguards Agreement (CSA).[8] The undeclared program consisted of activities that Iran was either legally required to disclose to the IAEA but did not or work that it was absolutely forbidden to pursue in accordance with Iran's NPT commitment not to pursue nuclear weapons. In this undeclared program, separate lines of work—some involving Atomic Energy Organization of Iran (AEOI) scientists and others involving personnel from the Ministry of Defense and Iranian Revolutionary Guard Corps (IRGC)—pushed forward Iran's understanding of nuclear science and the capabilities to use it.

The United States and some of its partners were sufficiently aware of this line of effort—though not necessarily its full extent or who was involved—to be concerned about Iran's nuclear program. On this basis, the United States and its partners discouraged nuclear cooperation with Iran through the 1980s and 1990s. Coincident with this effort, the United States also imposed its own domestic sanctions on Iran for a variety of bad acts, such as support for terrorism. This effort began in earnest in 1984, the year Iran was named a State Sponsor of Terrorism. The United States imposed a sweeping embargo on all U.S. trade with Iran in 1995. But because U.S.-Iranian trade had never again approached the levels of significance that marked the pre-revolution relationship, the impact on Iran from this step was muted.

For this reason, the United States also tried to leverage its own economic position to discourage other countries from pursuing new business with Iran. This took the form of the Iran-Libya Sanctions Act of 1996 (ILSA), which targeted new investments in Iran's oil and gas sectors (as well as those of Libya). ILSA was the real start of the U.S. sanction campaign that culminated in the Joint Comprehensive Plan of Action (JCPOA) in 2015, though it was an inauspicious beginning. For the rest of the world, U.S. hostility to Iran—and its nuclear program as well—was assumed to be only a result of the overall negative U.S.-Iran relationship post 1979, a product of mutual recriminations, the hostage taking at the U.S. embassy, and the resulting break in diplomatic relations between the countries. Thus, instead of starting international bandwagoning, ILSA was widely condemned around the world as an extraterritorial application of U.S. law. The European Union was particularly aggrieved, as ILSA became law coincident with a similarly aggressive set of U.S. sanctions related to Cuba (named the Helms-Burton Act after its sponsors). The EU both announced the intention to file a grievance with the World Trade Organization and adopted new legislation that effectively forbade any EU legal person from complying with non-EU sanctions law (Council Regulation No 2271/96 of 22 November 1996). The Clinton administration negotiated an arrangement with the EU to deal with these challenges to U.S. sanctions, effectively shelving implementation of ILSA with respect to European companies so long as the United States and Europe cooperated to deal with the challenges presented by Iran.[9]

Only when confronted with unambiguous evidence of Iran's illicit activities did most of the world come to understand what Iran was doing and the threat presented by an unimpeded Iranian nuclear program. This realization began dawning in 2002 when the National Council of Resistance of Iran (NCRI, a dissident group associated with the Mujahadeen el Kaliq, a U.S.-designated terrorist group until 2012) announced at a press briefing the uncovering of two clandestine Iranian nuclear facilities. The first was a massive, "cut and cover" bunker installation at a place called Natanz, where Iran intended to build a 50,000 uranium centrifuge plant. The second was a heavy-water production plant at a place called Arak; heavy water can be used to moderate nuclear reactions for a type of nuclear reactor that also happens to be an effective producer of weapons-usable plutonium. At this point, Iran faced a critical choice: come clean or attempt to sweep under the carpet all of its past illicit work. Iran chose the latter, beginning a more active game of cat and mouse with the IAEA and the larger international community.

The Predicate of the Post-1996 Sanctions Campaign

My initial part in the Iranian nuclear drama was modest. I joined the Pacific Northwest National Laboratory (PNNL) in June 2003 as a Nonproliferation Graduate Fellow, based at the National Nuclear Security Administration (NNSA) of the U.S. Department of Energy (DOE). This program, like others, sought to bring early career professionals into the government, in this instance focused on managing the challenge of the spread of weapons of mass destruction. The fellowship program had its origins in the need of the Energy Department to staff new positions to support cooperative threat-reduction programs with the former Soviet Union. But, in time, the needs of the department prompted an expansion of the program and its writ.

I served as a special assistant to an assistant deputy administrator at DOE/NNSA. My task was, in essence, to be the grease that permitted the real professionals to do their jobs, while learning all that I could about the department, its mission, and my chosen area of specialization. Of course, this position also meant that I was available for whatever else DOE/NNSA might require.

Starting in December 2003, this included serving on the team that helped to dismantle Libya's nuclear weapons program under the landmark agreement struck between Libya, the United States, and the United Kingdom. My job on this team began with the mixture of joy and pain familiar to all interns: photocopying. In my case, I was photocopying sensitive documents retrieved from Libya to permit further analysis throughout the U.S. government. My participation in Libya-related efforts led me to be invited to join the DOE/NNSA team working on broader issues of nuclear noncompliance, such as those ongoing with North Korea and Iran. Over the next two years, I took on greater responsibility as an action officer at DOE/NNSA for the Iran file, including—in 2005–2006—participating in the development and delivery of technical briefings on the Iranian nuclear program to foreign governments around the world.

This was part of the U.S. government's overall strategy to explain to the rest of the international community the severity of the threat posed by Iran's activities. Here, the United States faced a variety of challenges, many of which centered on the credibility lost by the U.S. government over Iraq.

First, though the IAEA had made public some information concerning previously undeclared nuclear activities in Iran, a substantial basis for U.S. pressure was in its belief that Iran was actively pursuing a nuclear weapon outright, rather than just technologies that could enable the production of nuclear weapons at some point. However, unfounded U.S. assertions over the existence of weapons of mass destruction (WMD) in Iraq cast a deep shadow over international perceptions of the U.S. intelligence community. Many U.S. partners expressed doubts about the U.S.'s official conviction that Iran's nuclear program was irretrievably destined to result in nuclear weapons. They were prepared to accept some of Iran's arguments, especially in the absence of any direct, unambiguous evidence of Iranian nuclear weapons research. What the

IAEA found in Iran could support weapons production, to be sure, but it could also support civil nuclear energy. That Iran had failed to fulfill its obligations under the NPT was fairly clear and obvious, but Iran's argument that U.S. hostility and dissuasion of even declared, public, civil nuclear cooperation with Iran throughout the 1980s and 1990s forced the Iranians to go underground was persuasive to many international audiences. Second, though the invasion of Iraq had demonstrated U.S. war-fighting capability, U.S. failure to secure Iraq after the invasion and subsequent trouble in restoring order to the country created a sufficient drain on U.S. resources—when combined with the ongoing conflict in Afghanistan—that there was doubt in the U.S. ability to mount a third military offensive in the region and even more doubt that it would be prudent to do so. And, third, there was enough bad blood between the United States and many of its allies, particularly in Europe, over the entire matter of the invasion of Iraq that partner support for further U.S. military activity was impossible to assume.

The U.S. approach was to take a dramatically different tack with Iran than we had with Iraq, relying on the reports of international inspectors rather than those of intelligence officers to make the case that Iran was up to no good. Iran helped. From 2002 to 2005, Iran selectively disclosed parts of its nuclear program, usually just prior to having them exposed by the IAEA or others. But in these disclosures, Iran admitted to having conducted a wide range of nuclear activities that, per its Safeguards Agreement with the IAEA and pursuant to its NPT obligations, Iran should have declared years before. This included activities at a variety of locales in which undeclared nuclear work had taken place using undeclared nuclear materials. These admissions were documented in an IAEA report issued on November 15, 2004, at the request of the United States and its partners in September 2004.[10] Though the listing is technical in nature, a pattern of direct Iranian efforts

34

to undertaken sensitive nuclear activities far from the watchful eye of international inspectors is discernible:

86. As assessed in light of all information available to date, these failures can now be summarized as follows:

(a.) Failure to report:

    (i) the import of natural uranium in 1991, and its subsequent transfer for further processing;

    (ii) the activities involving the subsequent processing and use of the imported natural uranium, including the production and loss of nuclear material where appropriate, and the production and transfer of waste resulting therefrom;

    (iii) the use of imported natural UF6 for the testing of centrifuges at the Kalaye Electric Company workshop in 1999 and 2002, and the consequent production of enriched and depleted uranium;

    (iv) the import of natural uranium metal in 1993 and its subsequent transfer for use in laser enrichment experiments, including the production of enriched uranium, the loss of nuclear material during these operations and the production and transfer of resulting waste;

    (v) the production of UO2, UO3, UF4, UF6 and ammonium uranyl carbonate (AUC) from imported depleted UO2, depleted U3O8 and natural U3O8, and the production and transfer of resulting wastes; and

    (vi) the production of natural and depleted UO2 targets at ENTC and their irradiation in TRR, the subsequent processing of those targets, including the separation of plutonium, the production and transfer of resulting waste, and the storage of unprocessed irradiated targets at TNRC.

(b.) Failure to declare:
> (i) the pilot enrichment facility at the Kalaye Electric Company workshop; and
> (ii) the laser enrichment plants at TNRC and the pilot uranium laser enrichment plant at Lashkar Ab'ad.

(c.) Failure to provide design information, or updated design information, for:
> (i) the facilities where the natural uranium imported in 1991 (including wastes generated) was received, stored and processed (JHL, TRR, ENTC, waste storage facility at Esfahan and Anarak);
> (ii) the facilities at ENTC and TNRC where UO2, UO3, UF4, UF6 and AUC from imported depleted UO2, depleted U3O8 and natural U3O8 were produced;
> (iii) the waste storage at Esfahan and at Anarak, in a timely manner;
> (iv) the pilot enrichment facility at the Kalaye Electric Company workshop;
> (v) the laser enrichment plants at TNRC and Lashkar Ab'ad, and locations where resulting wastes were processed and stored, including the waste storage facility at Karaj; and
> (vi) TRR, with respect to the irradiation of uranium targets, and the facility at TNRC where plutonium separation took place, as well as the waste handling facility at TNRC.

(d.) Failure on many occasions to cooperate to facilitate the implementation of safeguards, as evidenced by extensive concealment activities.[11]

Paragraphs later, the IAEA offered the conclusion that, in the end, set the terms of conflict between the United States, its partners, and Iran until the initial nuclear deal was reached in 2013: "All the declared nuclear material in Iran has been accounted for, and therefore such material is not diverted to prohibited activities. The Agency is, however, not yet in a position to conclude that there are no undeclared nuclear materials or activities in Iran."[12] This same conclusion was offered by the IAEA in its reports on Iran's nuclear program through the subsequent years of IAEA investigations, and will persist until the IAEA is able to verify Iran's nuclear declarations fully (a process that—even with the provisions of the JCPOA intact for their full duration—could take another decade given the extent of Iran's undeclared work over the years).

Under the terms of Iran's CSA and the IAEA Statute, Iran's failure to provide the appropriate declarations and provide for inspections was grounds for a finding by IAEA that Iran was out of compliance with its obligations. Under paragraph XII.C of the IAEA statute, "the inspectors shall report any non-compliance to the Director General who shall thereupon transmit the report to the Board of Governors. The Board shall call upon the recipient State or States to remedy forthwith any non-compliance which it finds to have occurred. The Board shall report the non-compliance to all members and to the Security Council and General Assembly of the United Nations."[13] Upon receiving such a report, the UN Security Council and General Assembly could then decide how to respond.

It was on the basis of these verified, IAEA-reported Iranian violations that the United States sought to pursue international action. The United States and other countries greeted this report as a validation of their concerns about the nature of Iran's nuclear program, particularly in that IAEA Director General Mohamed El-Baradei, whose adversarial relationship with the George W. Bush administration over Iraq was public knowledge, issued it.

Though the United States had some ambition of reporting Iran to the UN Security Council based on November 2004 report, that report was issued amid negotiations that were ongoing between the members of the so-called EU-3 (France, Germany, and the

United Kingdom) over the terms of an Iranian suspension of its most significant nuclear activities. This suspension was intended to replace an earlier one, agreed to in October 2003 but fractured in subsequent months over a fundamental disagreement about key terms, such as the extent of the nuclear stand-down Iran was supposed to make. The EU-3 used the report and the threat of U.S. pressure to convince Iran to return to a more complete suspension of its fuel cycle activities and to the negotiating table.

However, this suspension too came under pressure, this time at the hands of political changes in Tehran. In June 2005, Mahmoud Ahmadinejad was elected president of Iran. The president of Iran is subordinate to the position of Supreme Leader, held since 1989 by Ayatollah Ali Khamenei. Consequently, the Iranian president does not have complete autonomy or full executive authority. But it is an important role, both from the standpoint of offering Iranians a sense of democratic control over their government institutions (though the degree to which this sense is real is subject to continual debate by observers and academics) and from the perspective of day-to-day government operations. On August 1, 2005, the Iranian government informed the IAEA that it was restarting some of the uranium conversion–related activities that had been suspended pursuant to the arrangement with the Europeans agreed in November 2004. Ahmadinejad was inaugurated on August 3. The Iranian Foreign Ministry declared the EU-3's negotiating offer for a long-term comprehensive solution "not acceptable" three days later, and activities commenced at Iran's uranium conversion facility at Esfahan on August 8.[14]

After a flurry of diplomatic activity—in which many delegations to the IAEA tried in vain to convince Iran to return to its suspension—the IAEA Board of Governors adopted a resolution on September 24, 2005, finding Iran in noncompliance with its nuclear obligations under the IAEA Safeguards Agreement.[15] A formal report to the UNSC was delayed until a later date so as to permit continued diplomatic initiatives, but it was clear to the United States (and to many others) that the Iranian government was committed to a more confrontational course of action. That night, the U.S. delegation celebrated a significant step forward in the campaign to address U.S. concerns with Iran's nuclear activities, but it was a celebration tinged with the reality that an IAEA resolution would not itself accomplish this goal. Instead of an ending, the IAEA Board of Governors' decision signaled the beginning of a much more involved, pressure-infused diplomatic campaign.

On to Sanctions

The IAEA Board of Governors voted to report Iran to the UN Security Council for its nuclear violations on February 4, 2006, after the Iranian government restarted uranium enrichment activities in January 2006. This proved to be the final straw for governments which, to date, had been giving Iran the benefit of the doubt and space to make a return to the EU-3-led diplomatic process. The vote to report Iran to the UN Security Council was lopsided, with twenty-seven members of the thirty-five-seat Board voting in favor of the report. Only Cuba, Syria, and Venezuela stood with Iran.[16] Russia and China voted in favor, and Iran now appeared isolated in the UN Security Council.

George W. Bush's State of the Union address given just days before the IAEA Board's February 4 vote made clear that "America will continue to rally the world to confront" the threats presented by Iran, including "its nuclear ambitions." President Bush declared that "the nations of the world must not permit the Iranian regime to gain nuclear weapons" and a statement issued by the president of the UN Security Council at the end of March 2006 underscored that the UNSC would remain seized of this matter until Iran complied with its nuclear obligations.[17]

But translating international interest into international action was easier said than done. The Bush administration decided to pursue an international sanctions path against Iran, convinced that UN-level action was a critical component of any successful sanctions effort (as the right UNSC language would require all UN member states to comply). But the other permanent members of the UN Security Council—whose veto-holding powers could preclude the adoption of UNSC sanctions—demanded a quid pro quo for consideration of UN sanctions: that Iran be first offered a clear choice between a package of incentives and the threat of an agreed list of sanctions.[18] The choice was conveyed by EU High Representative for Common Foreign and Security Policy Javier Solana on June 6, 2006, on behalf of the Permanent Five members of the Security Council—China, France, Russia, the United Kingdom, and the United States—and Germany, an arrangement that became known as the P5+1.[19] Through it starting in 2006, the United States and its partners sought to create a path for Iran to accept a diplomatic resolution to the crisis by combining an offer of negotiations with the threat of sanctions.

Iran was given two months to respond positively to the P5+1's offer, a decision made stark with the adoption of UNSCR 1696 at the end of July 2006. Iran's response on August 22, 2006, was contemptuous of the P5+1 incentives package, though Iran indicated it would be amenable to further talks with the P5+1.

By this time, I had moved from the DOE to the State Department, taking up my duties as one of the senior officers responsible for Iran's nuclear program in the Bureau of International Security and Nonproliferation. The State Department was as dismissive of Iran's counteroffer as the Iranians were of the P5+1 package, seeing little in the Iranian response—described as vague and rambling by one official—to commend it.[20] Instead, we began working on the options for a UNSC resolution that would impose sanctions on the Iranian nuclear program; my own primary responsibility was to assemble the list of individuals and entities to target in the resolution.

The P5+1 package from June 2006 offered some help in framing possible sanctions, which were to focus on Iran's nuclear and missile programs, its access to sensitive nuclear or missile-related goods, and the individuals and entities involved in running the nuclear and missile programs. There was consideration of wider, economic sanctions within the U.S. government, but consultations with the other members of the P5+1 suggested that these would be out of reach early on in the process.

However, there was little confidence within the U.S. government that UN sanctions would turn the tide with Iran (and, in fact, in some quarters outright disdain for the idea that sanctions in general would be useful). I recall a common view was that UN sanctions would never go far enough to affect Iranian thinking, let alone their strategic perception of the utility of a nuclear weapons option which was—at the time—assumed to be part of their ongoing research program. This mindset changed somewhat after the adoption of UNSCR 1737 on December 23, 2006, when it became clear that the Iranians were perturbed both by the adoption of measures targeting them and the fact that Russia and China joined in support of 1737's adoption. At that point, senior U.S. government officials suggested that the individual value of particular measures was secondary to the adoption of new sanctions altogether. The United States began to contemplate a persistent series of UNSC resolutions, coming like clockwork after every report by the IAEA Director General that Iran remained in noncompliance with both the requirements of the UNSC—which included the suspension of all of Iran's uranium enrichment, reprocessing and heavy water–related activities—and its NPT obligations. The tempo and the constant international condemnation had their own value to be exploited.

But there was also recognition in the United States that public, political pressure would be fleeting and that real economic pressure from the UNSC may be difficult to deliver even if Russia and China were supportive of sanctions in principle. The United

States was also considering alternative ways of bringing together the international community, building on the lessons of ILSA.

This translated into a far more serious effort to impose innovative new sanctions on Iran's economy by targeting the interconnections between it and the rest of the world. Such sanctions would be efficient—omitting as a direct result the sort of humanitarian catastrophe that came from the Iraq sanctions program—while also keeping the decision making in the hands of the United States. Predating the UNSC process, the first action was the July 1, 2005, authorization of new financial sanctions against those involved in the proliferation of WMD by President Bush in Executive Order 13382. This order specifically authorized the secretary of the treasury, in consultation with the secretary of state, to freeze the assets of WMD proliferators. Perhaps more important, it facilitates the inclusion of such targeted individuals and entities on the Treasury Department's Specially Designated Nationals and Blocked Persons (SDN) list, which banks around the world use to screen against transactions that could involve illicit goods. Iran was a major target of this initiative, as is demonstrated by the fact that of the eight entities so designated first, four were Iranian.[21]

By the end of 2006, the United States had used the E.O. 13382 authority not only to expand the list of designated entities and individuals, but also to engage with banks and companies around the world diplomatically. Even without the formal legal requirement to do so, the United States sought to educate the world's business community of the dangers of doing business with Iran (and—as a result—to dry up Iran's ability to conduct such business altogether).[22] And, perhaps most important, we began to tie together the strategy of using a combination of pressures—multilateral, national, diplomatic—to persuade Iran to change course.

4

On Sanctions Imposition and Pain

LET'S TAKE A STEP back now and think about how sanctions imposition and the application of pain work on a strategic level. There are many different ways to evaluate political systems and economies, as well as the effects of steps taken by governments to influence them. Structured, academically rigorous approaches are available to scholars interested in such things (Drezner's *The Sanctions Paradox* and Lisa Martin's book *Coercive Cooperation* offer compelling modeling approaches for conducting such analysis). Once again, I commend these works as well as others listed in the bibliography for such analysis.

In my experience, however, many models fall short because of the intrinsic difficulty of modeling national reactions of highly specific governments to highly specific events and stimuli. Below, I offer an approach based on my practical experience, combining academic and personal observations about what works and how to evaluate effectiveness and efficiency.

Types of Sanctions

Sanctions-imposed hardship can take many forms. Experts often describe sanctions as economic tools—and, indeed, the most destructive sanctions do target economic interests—but economic sanctions should be properly considered a class of sanctions rather than their totality. Broadly speaking, I view sanctions as encompassing the following main types: diplomatic/political, military, technological, and economic. I consider each briefly in turn.

Diplomatic/Political Sanctions

These sanctions impose a cost to the target's standing, either diplomatically or politically (and, consequently, tend to be associated with state-level sanctions rather than those applied against individuals or entities). Associated measures include suspension of a state's ability to participate in international organizations or committees, denial of visa privileges and other travel-related impediments, and a reduction in the level of diplomatic relations between governments (such as the withdrawal of an ambassador, either temporarily—"for consultations"—or permanently). These sanctions do impose hardship on the target, but the cost is often more in terms of international reputation than it is in economic loss. Importantly, this is conceptually distinct from notions of diplomatic wrangling that all states engage in at some level or another. The key criterion to differentiate simple "diplomacy" from a "diplomatic sanction" is that there is a perceived, intentional, substantive cost or harm done to the target of the sanction. Put in terms of contrasting examples, one could see the gathering of a coalition to oppose a resolution being pushed by a particular government as "diplomacy." On the other hand, one could see the act of seeking to lower the status of diplomatic relations with those governments that vote contrary to the sanctioner's wishes as a "diplomatic sanction."

To some extent, Palestinians and their supporters in the Arab world have been trying to impose this class of sanctions against Israel for decades. In addition to advancing the cause of a separate Palestinian state, they have sought to put pressure on Israel by attacking it in multilateral bodies, undermining its legitimacy internationally and subjecting it to criticism for its treatment of Palestinians.

Military Sanctions

These sanctions deny access to military hardware and technical assistance. They can include outright global embargoes—such as those imposed by the UN Security Council (UNSC) against Iraq and Iran—as well as state-based decisions to either preclude or halt military cooperation. The target of these sanctions is military, with the idea being that the loss of preexisting access or cooperation creates political pressure on the target, as well as, perhaps if only in the long term, a strain on its military forces.

The United States has used this tool against adversaries and partners, responding—for example—to nondemocratic changes in government in Egypt and elsewhere by denying military sales for a period of time. Likewise, in 1974, the United States slapped an arms embargo on Turkey—a NATO ally and critical frontline state in the Cold War—in response to its invasion of Cyprus.

Technological Sanctions

This category encompasses providing specific goods (including goods that could support WMD programs) and technical support across the board. The objective of this class of sanctions is to impair the technological development of a country, either in specific ways (such as denial of assistance with the development of an important national resource or economic opportunity) or more generally. In this way, these measures present longer-term implications than other types of sanctions. That said, they are also more scalable and usable against individuals and entities, which can be denied access to exports or participation in various projects.

The sanctions imposed against Russia's oil and gas industry in 2014 are a case in point. Although the impact will—in time—become economic, the primary target is the technological capabilities of the country. Similarly, sanctions imposed on items going to and from North Korea and Iran (at least prior to January 2016) had this character, isolating the countries from items that could be used not only for nuclear and missile programs but also for a whole host of other applications. Put another way, this type of sanction can impair economic growth indefinitely by lowering a country's potential versus merely knocking the economy off its current trajectory. But the intended principal effect of the sanctions is to impair the technological development of the target in question.

Economic Sanctions

This category is the most used type of sanction, and, arguably, the one with the most immediate punch. It is divisible in a variety of ways, with particular measures targeting the financial vulnerabilities of one target and the tangible goods of another. The objective of these sanctions is to damage the target's ability to obtain and use economic resources, thus undermining its objectionable conduct directly—by depriving it of the opportunity and/or means to act—and inflicting punishment. These sanctions are also scalable, targeting both various elements of economic activity (e.g., financial linkages) and different types of actors (depriving individuals and entities of their access to markets, or depriving entire countries of the same).

Considering the significance of this class of sanctions, it is worth dwelling on two particular avenues for their application: trade-related measures and finance-related measures. Throughout history, the term *economic sanctions* was largely synonymous with trade sanctions, with particular items being prohibited from import or export. Financial sanctions, in contrast, are a relatively new specialization, taking advantage of the increasingly globalized nature of currency markets, financial flows, and insurance patterns. Financial sanctions concentrate less on the types of commodities or goods being traded and more on the modalities of their trade, in acknowledgment of the central nature of financial flows for underlying trade and—for the United States and Europe—the centrality of Western countries for financial flows. Starting in 2005–2006, the United States has used financial sanctions and the threat of being cut off from the U.S. financial system as a cudgel, scaring banks and other financial institutions away from business with risky jurisdictions. In 2014, as we will see in chapter 9, touching on Russia, this tool took an entirely new tack, targeting foreign-held Russian debt as a means of exerting pressure. Ultimately, it is debatable whether the force of this type of economic sanction derives from the nature of the tool—imperiling financial linkages—or from nature of the states that wield it. But it is certain that such instruments have power and are seen as an artful way of approaching economic sanctions without inherently preventing the transfer of otherwise legitimate goods. (For more on financial sanctions and their utility, see Juan Zarate's excellent book, *Treasury's War*.)

Of course, the separation of sanctions measures into different categories is a matter of personal preference, for only in the rarest of circumstances are sanctions regimes structured so that their measures fall cleanly into only one or two types. More often than not, when sanctions are imposed, the constituent measures cross boundaries in order to account for the peculiarities of targets and their vulnerabilities: a central tenet of this book is that precisely this type of careful thinking is necessary for sanctions to be an effective part of strategy. For example, as noted in the previous chapter, in 1996, the United States imposed sanctions against Iran that denied it access to U.S. technology for the liquefaction of natural gas, thereby denying Iran the ability to tap fully the export potential of this resource, of which Iran has the second-largest reserves in the world. The sanction began as a technological one, but—especially after 2010—it had dramatic economic consequences. On the other hand, not all technological sanctions are primarily economic in nature: for example, the United States also denied Iran access to dual-use items that have limited nonsensitive applications but are widely utilized in nuclear and other WMD-related projects.

But separating measures into these four categories helps clarify two main points: first, sanctions are a more diverse set of tools than commonly presented; and, second, a well-developed sanctions strategy will seek to apply pain using the full tool kit, potentially with some measures employed in different ways or at different times to take advantage of circumstances that develop. In the following chapter, I will discuss in further detail the full range of potential overlaps as presented in the case of Iran starting in 2007.

Pain and Sanctions in a Strategic Context

The application of pain against a sanctions target is sheer sadism unless it is connected to an expectation about what that pain will achieve and is matched with a readiness to stop inflicting pain when the sanctioning state's objectives are met. In my experience, a state usually decides to use sanctions in order to satisfy at least one of the following interests:

- to affect the behavior and capabilities of the sanctions target
- to demonstrate commitment on the part of the sanctioner to persevere (which is strengthened if the imposition of sanctions comes with a cost to the sanctioner as well as the sanctioned)
- to satisfy domestic or international constituents' or stakeholders' demands for either a specific response to whatever misbehavior is underway or, more generally, for someone to "do something"
- to demonstrate willingness to escalate pressure if the sanctions target does not change course

But even so, there is incredible diversity in how sanctions can be employed. Some sanctions regimes are imposed swiftly, with rapid escalation from initial steps to a comprehensive set of restrictions, as in the case of Iraq in the 1990s. Other sanctions regimes take longer to develop, as was the case with Iran, which—as noted—began in earnest as an international movement with the adoption of UNSC resolution 1737 in December 2006. There are advantages to each approach, depending on the nature of the target and its transgressions, the extent of its vulnerabilities, and the degree of international support for the imposition of sanctions.

The two cases we have already discussed offer useful contrasts in this regard. In both cases, the sanctions regimes started with a significant first step, leaving room for the sanctions to grow thereafter. The primary difference is that, for Iraq, the escalation took place over a dramatically shorter time period in part because of the exigent nature of the circumstances—an active invasion with power in the occupied territory being consolidated on a daily basis as opposed to a notional threat of nuclear weapons acquisition at some time in the future—provided the necessary level of international support for a robust reaction. As mentioned previously, the absence of an opportunity for incremental escalation—so sensible in anticipation of military conflict but ultimately damaging as part of a longer-term containment strategy—eventually contributed to sanctions fatigue and policy failure in Iraq.

Escalation is the currency of coercive diplomacy. Opponents must believe that you are not only prepared to go further, but that doing so is inevitable without resolution of the underlying problem. The implicit choice becomes: you can stop this now or suffer worse. Sanctions imposition fits this profile, with escalation taking the form of new measures targeting new sectors or an intensification of the pressure on already targeted sectors. In this regard, the time lag of sanctions imposition is an integral, operative part of the sanctions regime. We will see this in the following chapters, particularly when discussing the U.S. sanctions regime on Iranian oil sales to third countries.

Over time, pain is added to the sanctions regime, intensifying the negative consequences to the sanctioned party for continuing with its intransigence. Importantly, increased pain can come either as a result of *new* sanctions or from *existing* sanctions. States have the ability to ratchet up or down the pain that they apply via sanctions. In no circumstances, however, is pain infinite in its potentiality. At some point, there is no economy to sanction and no trade to deny. This situation could arise quickly or over a long period of time, but it is unrealistic to assume that it lies within the province of a sanctioning state to impose endless escalation of pain.

Assuming that this limit exists, the most intense, initial application of sanctions pain would still have an upper bound. This is meaningful because it also sets an upper bound to our expectations of what is possible. Sanctions pain is not a limitless source of leverage but rather a commodity that has particular value and currency. And at some point the utility of sanctions pain may also decrease, depending on the nature of a sanctioned country's resolve.

I will cover the issue of resolve in greater detail in the next chapter. But it is important to clarify that just as no two persons perceive pain in the same fashion, no two countries perceive sanctions in the same fashion. It is clear that the sender perceives pain differently than the target. What's less obvious is that one's perception of how painful the pain is can also vary depending on who one is. Here, we speak to the issue of mirror imaging, which has been a known problem in intelligence community analysis for decades but also merits consideration here.

Let's simplify this by talking about a common government problem—unemployment. All governments likely prefer full employment to massive unemployment. Employed citizens tend to be happier citizens, more satisfied with their government and its performance, and less inclined to revolt (in whatever fashion is feasible depending the nature of the host government system and local culture or society). Unemployed citizens are, by extension, probably less happy citizens, less satisfied with their lot in life and the performance of their government. But beyond these generalizations, there are infinite variations in how populations might react to an unemployment crisis.

The U.S. election of 2016, ironically, helps to show this distinction. As of Election Day 2016, unemployment was back below levels that preceded the Great Recession of 2008–2009.[1] San Francisco Federal Reserve President John Williams had declared in May 2016 that the United States was "basically back at full employment."[2] Putting aside all other considerations, this situation logically should have resulted in a more relaxed voter posture on economic issues, permitting voters to focus on other issues in choosing which presidential candidate to support. However, as the political website *FiveThirtyEight* demonstrated shortly after the election, voting positions differed significantly based on relative considerations of job security, with those in economically weaker positions less inclined to view the U.S. economy as well run (and thereby more willing to choose a candidate with a business background and outsider brand).[3] The point is that even within one extremely prosperous country, there were sharp cleavages in public perception of economic strength, the risk of unemployment, and how to respond. And, consequently, the level of analysis necessary to understand the effect of unemployment on decision making—even at the level of the average voter—was far more granular that a simple observation would permit.

In a country with a tradition of full employment or even government guarantee of a job, discontent with unemployment may be greater than in a country where jobs have been scarce for generations and the economic situation is dog-eat-dog. Whether the two countries in these examples have domestic situations that permit dissent is irrelevant for our purposes: the point is that unemployment in the first country is logically a greater source of dissatisfaction than in the second.

Now let's layer on the problem of sanctions, starting with the proposition that sanctions are imposed on both countries and designed in such a way as to force layoffs in export-intensive industries. Regardless of various individual factors such as population size, it is logical to posit that people in the country with traditions and rules supporting full employment will be more upset by the imposition of these sanctions than the country in which unemployment is the norm, or where the social safety net is such that unemployment is less meaningful.

And now let's posit instead that the country with a tradition of full employment is the one imposing sanctions generating unemployment on the country with no such tradition. The policymakers in the sending country would doubtless assume at the gut level, even taking aside their own knowledge of the target country, that such sanctions measures would have a devastating impact on the target country and its internal cohesion. But this may not be the case at all; the sanctioned country may well simply shrug off the assault.

This issue highlights a central challenge of sanctions enforcement—knowing the nature of your opponent—as well as a risk that the sanctioning country may determine that "sanctions" simply don't work against the target. In our short hypothetical exercise, the problem was not that "sanctions" failed to work but rather that the target country did not feel as much pain as the sanctioning country intended because the sanctioning country did not really understand the full nature of its target and how the measure selected would work.

A way to work through this problem lies in understanding how pain is applied and felt. It is useful to know that pain imposition can be ratcheted up or down depending on circumstances and that incremental escalation can be achieved in concert with changes in international environment. But this is less useful if it is impossible to know whether the pain is having its intended effect.

Assessing the Level of Pain Applied and Felt

Pain should be measured in relation to the identified values and vulnerabilities of the target country and how much the sanctions cost the target, rather than out of an absolute assessment of precisely what happens when sanctions are imposed. In my view, this means that a standard model that could give real guidance would be impossible to develop without knowing some national specifics. But that's the point. Sanctions should be tailored; they usually wear poorly directly off the rack.

An individualized measurement approach would ultimately focus on assessing the sanctioned state's national priorities and self-image and how best to injure them. But critical factors that would contribute to this assessment could include the following eight points (which are not in order of importance, as this depends on the country in question).

The Nature of the Target Country's
Political Institutions

Is the country a democracy or an autocracy? Do the various political groups in the country have a say in its affairs or does a ruling clique make the decisions? Answering these questions is important for a clear understanding of whether political forces can be galvanized to create internal pressure as a result of externally applied pain. All states being somewhat different, the key factor is not whether a country can be classified with a one-word identifier but rather whether the various elements of power can be described in sufficient detail to articulate who holds what power in that system. North Korea and ISIS are particularly extreme examples of this phenomenon. North Korea's governance structures are sufficiently opaque that it is unclear whether, outside of Kim Jong Un, there are leaders to be influenced. ISIS, by contrast, may have a variety of potential pressure points in the form of many different centers of government gravity, but its very diffusion—combined with the zealous nature of its construction—bedevils sanctions pressure as a means of influence. Instead, as was shown in the early part of 2016, financial pressure on ISIS through the direct destruction of its assets may be more meaningful if orchestrated as a means of denying capabilities rather than changing ISIS policy.

The Existing Macroeconomic and Financial System,
and Its Vulnerabilities

Is the country an advanced economy, integrated into the rest of the international system? Or is it an emerging economy, still finding its place? These distinctions matter greatly, as they speak to the degree to which an economy is itself vulnerable to international forces. They also can inform an effective analysis of whether the country can push back on sanctions, imposing its own costs on sanctioners. Beyond that, important subsidiary questions merit examination, including the degree to which the economy is open or closed, private or state controlled. Economic pressure, in particular, requires a clear-eyed understanding of where and against which groups the sanctions pain will be felt. Economic inequality is another related factor that ought to be contained in the assessment.

The Nature of Its Trade Relationships

Although closely related to the previous topic, assessment of this factor should focus on how vulnerable a country is to different forms of economic coercion. If a country is dependent on one or two other countries for all of its trade, then the sanctions regime might focus on applying broad pressure against a narrow subset of the economy. If, by contrast, a country is open to business around the world, then it may be easier to instead target one or two particular sectors and seek to scale back the target country's overall ability to conduct business in those sectors. Here, too, consideration must be given to the nature of the sector and the companies that operate in it, both for the target country and for those doing business with it. If the primary avenue for trade lies in state-to-state enterprises, then direct sanctions pressure on both the target country and its trading partners at a governmental level would be prudent. By contrast, if the target country's international business is conducted largely by and between private-sector entities, then the method of applying pressure could change, possibly focusing instead on informal, private means of applying pressure by simply convincing foreign companies to withdraw from the affected sectors (as occurred with Iran from 2006 to 2010). Moreover, if a country's economy is closed (or near enough as makes no difference), the application of sanctions pressure via economic sources will be inherently more difficult to arrange, execute, and sustain with any significance. A state in autarky may be weak from an economic theory perspective but strong from the perspective of avoiding externally applied economic pressure.

Cultural Values

Is the country's population materially motivated or not? Does its population subscribe to a religion with a history of martyrdom? Are the United Nations and multilateral institutions important sources of pride and legitimacy? Such questions can help explain responses to the imposition of sanctions pain and calibrate expectations for what kind of pain may be necessary to overcome resolve. They can also help steer the type of sanction to use. A country that prizes the UN system (such as East Timor, which owes its existence in part to the United Nations) might be more affected by sanctions limiting its UN voting rights and normal status than a country far more dismissive of the United Nations and similar institutions. Cultural values can be overinterpreted, however, and ought to be evaluated with care. Simply because a country has a primary religion that embraces pain and sacrifice is no guarantee that sanctions-driven pain won't touch the population or its government, just as a long historical memory is no protection against present hardship. Everyone's grandfather may have walked to school in ten feet of snow, uphill both ways, but knowledge of this experience is less salient when someone is shoveling two feet of snow on a blustery day. Cultural values and experience are important and should be factored in, but they are neither deterministic nor an excuse to discount other elements of analysis.

Indeed all too often, in my experience, those utilizing such values as an argument for or against a position are adhering to stereotypes in order to avoid complicated assessment. The debate over the form of sanctions to take against Iran provides a case in point. Some suggested that because Shi'ism is a religion that praises martyrdom and includes practices such as self-flagellation, Iranians were incapable of responding to economic sanctions. Of course, this is a gross exaggeration of both religious practice and Iranian personal experience; one might just as well argue that since Catholics revere martyred saints, they too are incapable of responding to economic sanctions. I urge consideration of cultural factors but also caution that we delineate between meaningful elements of national consciousness on one hand, and sentiment and stereotype on the other.

Recent History

Has the country been at war for decades or experienced a long period of peace? Even such a simple question can help create a picture of what kind of sanctions pain may be required to shake the country's leadership into pursuing a new course. Moreover, countries can also emerge from such situations with vastly different views of what pain they can accept going forward. A victorious country that underwent some privation could be more resilient than one that expended vast sums of blood and treasure for a failed cause. And, of course, war is not the only critical element of recent history: other events, such as political upheaval, natural disasters, and economic recession, are also key.

Demography

Is the population balanced between old and young, male and female? Or is it excessively young or old, skewed toward one gender group or the other? Some forms of economic pressure, in particular, are more effective in targeting a young population versus an older one, such as sanctions that cause unemployment in the kind of manufacturing and industrial jobs that young people might lose faster and never regain. Travel bans, especially those restricting the freedom of movement of young, urban populations and students, might likewise be more troublesome for some countries than others. Knowing the population's composition can help ensure that targeting is as effective as possible.

Access to Outside Sources of Information

Can the country in question access external sources of information so as to overcome national propaganda services and the local rumor mill? Are parts of the population free to access such information and question the arguments made by their government representatives? Or would such knowledge be considered a capital crime? There are benefits to a sanctioner from widespread access to a number of information sources, but knowledge of the situation on the ground is imperative so as to help the sanctioner understand the mindset of the population and leadership in experiencing sanctions.[4]

Sanctions Construction Questions

Are the measures that may be achievable also enforceable? An example of an issue that could arise under this topic is physical geography: is the country a small island that is easily embargoed or a large country with wide-ranging borders that are hard to monitor? Another issue is the value of a country in the global economy or politics. Shades of the answers to these questions can be found in other parts of this proposed assessment, but conducting a separate, focused query on whether enforcement can be meaningfully undertaken is also warranted to ensure the very concept of sanctions makes sense.

Iraq and Iran provide studied contrasts for such a national assessment-based approach. In Saddam's Iraq, we had a country that was ruled by an autocratic strongman who made very little attempt to hide his approach to governance. The Iraqi population had little opportunity to challenge government decisions and there were grave consequences for doing so. Saddam ruled substantial parts of his country through terror, including the use of chemical weapons against the Kurds to the north and the Shi'a to the south. The Iraqi economy was state run and oil dependent, leading to chronic underemployment. By the time sanctions were imposed, Iraq's recent history was one of war, with Iraq having fought Iran for eight years and then the United States and its partners for six weeks. Access to economic information was a state secret. And prior to the Internet, the average Iraqi's ability to access foreign-generated information was fairly limited. Radio and satellite TV broadcasts did exist but were also subject to jamming, which hindered the ability of the average Iraqi to understand the purpose of the pressure they easily perceived.

Iran in the 2000s appears quite distinct. Although ruled by an authoritarian system, Iran's government operates on a consensus-building approach, in which a variety of stakeholders can express their views and concerns. Further, the Iranian sense of government legitimacy flows from the Iranian revolution, in which power was passed from an autocratic strongman into—if in name only to some degree—the hands of the people. Censorship and the threat of reprisal exist, but access to external news sources and information (as well as the relative ease of Iranian citizen travel outside of the country) ensures that even politically marginalized points of view are understood within the country. The Iranian economy is also oil dependent and government controlled, but increasingly diverse and privatized, as well. Iran has prioritized the development of new industries to reduce its reliance on a single commodity. The Iranian population is relatively young, in part a consequence of the military conflict with Iraq in which hundreds of thousands of Iranians died. Its government leadership is also more religious than that of Iraq, and it is affiliated with the Shi'a branch of Islam, which has an affinity for self-sacrifice and martyrdom, as well as the nobility of resistance.

From a sanctions design perspective, one can deduce a few lessons from even this superficial treatment of the national characteristics of each country. For example, one could make an educated guess that targeting the population of Iraq might have less value than targeting the population of Iran because the Iraqi people have relatively less stake and say in how decisions are made in the country. Likewise, sanctioning Iran's private sector would theoretically have more coercive power than sanctioning the Iraqi private sector. That said, both countries' reliance on oil as their primary economic driver suggests that oil-related sanctions would be effective in either case. A key issue for ensuring the effectiveness of sanctions against both countries would be communication: ensuring that the population understood the complicity of their respective governments in creating the sanctions problem. Although there is censorship in both countries, Iran (due to the wider penetration of modern communications technology) is probably an easier lift for this communication challenge than Iraq (a challenge that a twenty-year difference in global telecommunications development has accentuated). On the other hand, Iranians could also believe that their own sense of empowerment by the government gives them a stake in the country, which might consequently increase their willingness to stand with the government in defying the rest of the world.

A similar exercise can be conducted with respect to other countries using a similar logical framework. The purpose in doing so is to first identify the sanction categories that would have an impact and then identify particular vulnerabilities within it. Categories vary in significance depending on the vulnerabilities targeted.

Let's take a practical example. Prohibiting arms transfers to countries that do not frequently import them has far less effect than such an action taken against countries which are major importers of arms; that said, those that do not import arms because they are primarily exporters of them might still find that a comprehensive arms embargo bites significantly. For example, the United States is largely untouchable with respect to the possibility of military sanctions. Its vast domestic production capacity gives it considerable independence, although the sourcing of some constituent raw materials may create hindrances. But an arms embargo against the United States is fairly insignificant as an instrument, just as it would be against any other state that possesses a robust domestic arms industry.

One cannot make the same bold statement with respect to economic sanctions against the United States. Though counterintuitive given both the size of the U.S. economy and its own weight internationally, as I have written elsewhere, the United States is itself vulnerable to economic disruption from the outside.[5] For example, in 2012, the Federal Reserve issued a paper that noted the following:

> The income received on the US external position plays an important role in one of the biggest issues confronting international macroeconomists—the sustainability (or lack thereof) of the US current account deficit. Net income receipts, which equaled 33 percent of the goods and services balance in 2010, provide a significant stabilizing force for the current account. Future sustainability will depend, in part, on the persistence of these net income receipts.[6]

Implicitly, this conclusion suggests that a denial of U.S. access to foreign markets would have a profoundly damaging impact on the U.S. current account balance and, with it, on the ability of the United States to maintain positive economic performance. It may not be possible to engineer such a set of sanctions given international politics, but this is a different question than whether such measures would hurt if achieved.

Moreover, some vulnerabilities may not be intuitively obvious, requiring either an analyst's special awareness of a country or insight from its own population. For example, although Pew polling suggests that Israelis generally have a low opinion of the United Nations (or did in 2013), this may not be the case for elites.[7] More than one Israeli diplomat reminded me during my time at the State Department that the role of the United Nations in Israel's formation means that UN condemnation of Israeli policy bites deeper than might be imagined. This lens in place, I have found myself much more understanding of why UN condemnation of Israel—or resolutions that Israeli officials argue undermine its security—hits such a nerve for the Israeli government. Iran also has demonstrated an interesting love/hate relationship with the United Nations, several times arguing that the United Nations has no jurisdiction over its nuclear program while simultaneously pursuing leadership roles on as many UN committees as it can obtain.

From my experience, therefore, the best starting place for sanctions design lies not in considering the tools available but rather in understanding the nature of the state. By fits and starts, it is how we brought the heat applied to the Iranian economy and government after 2006.

5

Pressure Begins on Iran

IN 2007, THE UNITED STATES sought to increase the pressure on Iran dramatically by convincing the rest of the world that the Iranian nuclear program was accelerating in direct violation of Iran's international obligations and in a manner that was likely to grant Iran a nuclear weapons option. The Iranians gave us plenty of ammunition, starting with the decision to restart uranium enrichment at the underground facility at Natanz. This decision permitted the United States to articulate clearly the decreasing opportunity to arrest Iran's nuclear program before it would be necessary to decide between preemptive military action and acquiescence to a de facto Iranian nuclear weapons capability. Our argument simplified quickly from "if the Iranians were to restart their uranium enrichment work, then . . ." to "every month Iran enriches uranium and expands its program, they get closer to nuclear weapons." In diplomacy, simplicity works.

Continuing Pressure Under President George W. Bush

That said, the specter of Iraq haunted U.S. efforts and complicated our ability to galvanize international cooperation early on. First, there was the prevailing (and, to some, open) question of whether our understanding of Iran's nuclear intentions was flat wrong. In early 2007, there were isolated, public references in IAEA reports about past Iranian nuclear weapons work but hardly anything conclusive. Moreover, uranium enrichment—like so many other sensitive nuclear activities—is not only permitted under the NPT but is also a guaranteed right in the opinion of some international readers. The United States did not share this interpretation and felt convinced that Iran's intentions were military in nature, but winning this argument was undoubtedly complicated by the legacy of Iraq, the discredited nature of U.S. intelligence on WMD, and the absence of clear proof that Iran was in fact developing a nuclear warhead.

Consequently, the strategy that evolved in 2007 was one that can be said to have loosely centered on three assumptions:

- There is enough evidence that Iran's nuclear program could be used to support nuclear weapons rather than nuclear power to create uncertainty in the minds of Iran's erstwhile international trading partners. Moreover, Iran's long legacy of bad acts and continuing support for terrorism and violations of human rights at home help create reputational risk in doing business with Iran.
- The reputational risk that foreign partners perceive is insufficient to prompt a wholesale departure from the Iranian economy, particularly given the number of contractual entanglements that might exist. Crude oil exports, natural gas purchases, and major investments will be hard to sever absent more compelling indications of bad acts. The resources they supply are too valuable, as are the profits

of the third-party companies involved (many of which are state owned or have strong ties to governments).

• Although a head-on approach to Iran's key national assets— such as its oil and gas industry—will be difficult to engineer, there are other ways of undermining those assets. Put another way, while going after the muscles of the Iranian body economic would be difficult, the tendons, ligaments, and joints were fair game and more susceptible to damage.

The United States spent 2007 and 2008, in particular, identifying all of that connective tissue.

The most obvious targets were Iran's links to international banking and its involvement in the international financial sector. In 2007, Iran was—by and large—a "normal" country for international finance. Of all the world's significant economies in 2007, only the United States had imposed direct limitations on Iran's ability to access its financial sector. Other countries had transaction- and issue-specific prohibitions; involvement in support for terrorism, money laundering, corruption, and similar such financial crimes were precluded on their own, separate substantive basis. But other countries did not see Iran itself as pervasively riddled with illicit activity and deserving of sanctions in its own right.

Consequently, the first U.S. task was to demonstrate the degree to which any business with Iran's banks ran the risk of contributing to its illicit activities. UNSCR 1737 provided significant support in this regard, as it prohibited (in operative paragraph 6) any service that might facilitate Iran's proliferation-sensitive nuclear activities or development of a nuclear weapon delivery system. Financial services were particularly called out. The United States used this to its advantage by highlighting the degree to which Iran's state-owned banks were involved in providing such financial services. In part on this basis (as well as specific information about its involvement in nuclear proliferation), the UNSC designated Iran's Bank Sepah in its next resolution, UNSCR 1747, adopted in March 2007.

This designation—as well as the accompanying designations of six members of the IRGC—allowed the United States to connect dots for international firms and ask a question that—to this point—was missing in the business discourse: Can you prove that you're not providing support to Bank Sepah or to the IRGC, including these officers? Banks around the world added Bank Sepah to their screening lists, as well as all of the rest of the UN-designated individuals and entities. More importantly, they started to probe into the extent of their knowledge of Iran's economy and their ties to it. They did not like what they found, particularly when the United States provided information (and imposed further sanctions) that outlined the degree to which other Iranian banks were taking up Sepah's slack and providing financial services to the IRGC and other actors in Iran. One of the most significant U.S. actions in this regard was the imposition of sanctions on the IRGC itself, Iran's Ministry of Defense and Armed Forces Logistics, Banks Melli and Mellat, and many other entities on October 25, 2007.[1] The press release outlined the degree to which Iran's banks were not only participating in but also complicit with the illicit activities of Iranian security services. The United States government took this declassified information and lobbied governments—and, more important—banks and companies to curtail their association with these entities and individuals.

Additionally, the United States saw other potential targets for the same strategy, essentially any other service provider that could not guarantee its noninvolvement in illicit Iranian activity. The next sector vulnerable to such pressure was transportation. Throughout 2007, the United States looked for opportunities to deny Iran access to shipping and transportation services that could facilitate illicit cargo. The argument sintered down to: Iran has spent the past twenty years exploiting the international economy and its transportation links to support its proliferation efforts. Can you prove that you're not involved?

The argument got boosts along the way, starting with the continuing IAEA exploration of Iran's nuclear procurement efforts
beginning in the 1980s. During the fall of 2007, the IAEA worked
with Iran to try to close lingering issues of past noncompliance,
setting aside the insurmountable problem of Iran's continuing
violations of its UNSC obligation to suspend enrichment and
other nuclear activities. The IAEA's investigation demonstrated
that Iran purposefully evaded international export controls for its
own purposes and took advantage of its integration in the global
economy to do so. Iran's defense was that international sanctions
precluded its ability to engage in normal commerce, requiring it
to enlist the services of at least one university to obtain necessary
components.[2] Iran essentially admitted to widespread sanctions
evasion, proving—from the U.S. perspective—that evasion was
not only happening but also that a sanctions compliance approach
dependent on avoiding links to explicitly designated entities could
be insufficient. And, true to form, Iran continued with this practice,
finding new intermediaries to purchase items that sanctions had
precluded. In this way, the Iranian government ensnared ever-larger
parts of its economy in illegitimate acts, essentially opening itself
up to a wider range of sanctions targeting; in struggling against
the sanctions regime, Iran made it easier to intensify the pressure
on its economy.

All the while, the United States sought to delegitimize otherwise
normal commerce with Iran. UNSCR 1747 was helpful in this
regard, calling for "states and international financial institutions
not to enter into new commitments for grants, financial assistance, and concessional loans, to the government of the Islamic
Republic of Iran, except for humanitarian and developmental
purposes."[3] The international financial institutions—the IMF and
World Bank, in particular—were already essentially walled off
from Iran programs on the basis of the U.S. voting strength and
ability to stop any projects from going forward. But by signaling
to states that extending support for trade and investment deals in

Iran was frowned upon, the UNSC accelerated Iran's separation from normal economic life.

UNSCR 1803—adopted in March 2008—amplified this problem for Iran, which was intentional on the part of the United States. We knew that obtaining UNSC support for major economic sanctions remained impossible. But we could see that our efforts to target the interconnections between Iran and the global economy were starting to complicate Iranian life—even if the Iranian economy had seen no significant drop in performance along the major economic indicators. Iranian GDP growth remained healthy, around 6.2–6.6 percent, and although inflation and unemployment were high, the IMF in 2008 predicted continued strong performance so long as oil prices remained high.[4] The IMF expressed concern that structural reforms were insufficient and that divestment by the state of its interest in various companies and entities was limited, in that they were mainly going into the hands of quasi-state actors (which subsequently appear likely to have been mostly IRGC-related enterprises). But the IMF saw no indication that imminent trouble was on the horizon for Iran.

The United States, however, saw things differently because Iran's access to the normal currents of international commerce was becoming constrained. As then Undersecretary of the Treasury Stuart Levey testified before the Senate Finance Committee on April 1, 2008: "the world's leading financial institutions have largely stopped dealing with Iran, and especially Iranian banks, in any currency. Foreign-based branches and subsidiaries of Iran's state-owned banks are becoming financial pariahs—threatening their viability—as banks and companies around the world resist dealing with them."[5]

In UNSCR 1803, the United States saw an opportunity to magnify these problems by focusing on three areas: financial services; shipping and transportation; and export credits and guarantees. The first two elements involved new language and authorities—such as an option for states to inspect shipping conducted by the Islamic Republic of Iran Shipping Lines (IRISL) and Iran Air Cargo—but their overall mindset was much in keeping with a two-year-old strategy: to undermine Iran's claim of normalcy and legitimacy, and to increase the sense of risk in international businesses and banks. By targeting export credits and guarantees, however, we looked to undermine the economic basis whereby business with Iran could be profitable within normal risk tolerances. Here, we took advantage of some knowledge of Iran and business practices with and within it.

It is no surprise to anyone with even a modicum of knowledge about Iran that, following the Iranian revolution, there was widespread concern among business operators that government actors could expropriate assets in Iran without warning; the fact that Prime Minister Mossadegh nationalized Iran's oil industry in 1953 was not lost on anyone operating in Iran's oil and gas sector, and of course Iran went even further in the aftermath of the Iranian Revolution. The Iranian Constitution explicitly conveys ownership of all oil and gas resources to the state. Oil and gas companies that did invest in Iran after the Revolution found their greatest difficulty was navigating this political reality while remaining profitable, not easy in a business that has been to some degree dependent on "booked" reserves to drive investment. Export credits and guarantees were used by governments around the world to provide some sense of protection to the companies that sought to do business in Iran anyway, essentially by putting the full faith and credit of their associated governments on the line in the event of an adverse political event in Iran. Even prior to the adoption of UN Security Council Resolution 1803, the German government had limited its willingness to extend export credits to businesses trading with Iran sharply.[6] After UNSCR 1803, this trend intensified even though the resolution did not legally prohibit credits or guarantees and merely called for vigilance. The European Union adopted a Common Position on August 7, 2008, that required restraint on the part of EU member states with respect to such credits and guarantees. Others noticed the shift and took similar steps, as the then chief economist of Australia's export credit agency also noted in August 2008.[7]

This came on top of banks being unwilling to lend to Iran or to businesses interested in operating in Iran. The result was that Iran had to find companies prepared to absorb the risk of business in Iran on their own, companies capable of obtaining other forms of risk insurance or self-finance. Levey later testified on October 6, 2009, that:

> Iran's foreign borrowing has sharply declined since 2006, a significant change from 2002 to 2005, when foreign credit growth to Iran outpaced that of the wider Middle East. External credit to Iran fell 18 percent between September 2006 and September 2008, in stark contrast to the 86 percent rise in external credit to the Middle East region during the same period. And, to the extent that Iranian firms have been able to replace lost credit with domestic credit, they are likely doing so at a much higher cost.[8]

Of course, this was not the end of the U.S. national sanctions campaign, which expanded to target insurance providers as well.[9] The United States sought to tie all types of services to the underlying potential illicit acts. In so doing, it spread the burden and risks of business with Iran to wider circles of the global economy. And to this point, the United States had acted without having actually impeded the sale of Iranian crude oil, still Iran's most vital natural resource and export revenue generator.

One key mechanism for achieving this new sanctions pressure was the enlistment of what we called the "Likeminded" in the development of their own sanctions regimes, which we dubbed "coordinated national measures." This project began small and in the shadow of Russia's invasion of Georgia in the summer of 2008, which ended negotiations around a successor UNSC resolution to

UNSCR 1803. Though some of the main elements of this successor resolution would find their way into resolution 1929 (adopted during the Obama administration), at the time, prospects were not high that the United States and Russia would work again on a substantive resolution that targeted Iran. UNSCR 1835 was adopted in September 2008, but it was largely rhetorical, serving as a capstone to the Bush administration's efforts and handing the ball off to the next administration.

But, through coordinated national measures, the United States sought to obtain some of the benefits of a UNSCR without having to go through the Russians and Chinese. At first, this effort largely resulted in a "démarche club," in which the United States and key partners—Germany, France, and the United Kingdom to start—would prepare messages for particular targets, pressing them to stop business in one area or another. Over time, the group expanded to include Italy, Japan, South Korea, Saudi Arabia, the United Arab Emirates, Canada, and Australia, as well as work to develop specific sanctions measures. During a series of senior-level meetings held in Rome, Ottawa, and Washington, the United States laid the groundwork for a sanctions onslaught to come under President Obama.

The Beginning of the Obama Administration

Most of what has been written about the early Obama administration's Iran policy fixates on the renewed offer of engagement made by President Obama both publicly and in a letter conveyed to Supreme Leader Khamenei in the spring of 2009. This effort was important, as it helped set the context for Iranian-American relations over the next eight years. It was a means of persuading the international community that the United States was taking the engagement track of P5+1 Iran policy seriously. Doing so had merit on its own, but it also served as a crucial component of the sanctions track that, if Iran refused to take advantage of Obama's kind offers for negotiations, would be even more important.

In fact, throughout the spring and summer of 2009, sanctions experts at the Departments of State and Energy were working away at developing further ideas for sanctions against Iran. As noted above, some of this work was already done: I had a list of sanctions ideas that I perpetually checked off as UNSCRs were adopted and national measures were imposed, and that I added to as new ideas occurred to us.

In fact, over the summer of 2009, the direction of the National Security Council and Secretary of State Clinton, the State Department began to develop specific baskets of sanctions measures, refining the options within them into one-page, simple proposals that described the sanctions measure, offered context about its value, advantages, and disadvantages, and conveyed a sense of how it could best be executed. This work was conducted under the direction of Ambassador Steve Mull, then serving as an at-large senior advisor of Under Secretary of State Bill Burns; I served as a deputy of sorts to Ambassador Mull, working with the rest of the State Department as well as with Treasury to flesh out these baskets of options. Our sanctions baskets covered Iran's energy, transportation, and financial sectors, as well as its nuclear program, arms industry, and diplomatic access to the outside world. These proposals were briefed to the NSC's Deputies Committee in September 2009, simultaneous with efforts to develop confidence-building measures that could be offered to Iran as part of a renewed diplomatic strategy. This latter effort included the Tehran Research Reactor (TRR) project, which was formally proposed to Iran in October 2009 (and which I also worked on). This project offered to provide nuclear fuel for the TRR in exchange for the removal from the country most of Iran's enriched uranium stockpile. From the U.S. perspective, this trade made good sense, as Iran would receive nuclear fuel that could not be easily used in nuclear weapons, while its creeping stock of more easily diverted material left the country.

Moreover, Iran would lose another reason to enrich uranium and the concept of foreign supply of nuclear fuel would be reaffirmed, damaging Iran's narrative that it could not count on international markets and had to have an indigenous capability.

Unfortunately, Iranian politics damned this offer. Iran's lead negotiator, Saeed Jalili, originally expressed interest in this proposal when tabled by the IAEA and Bill Burns. In fact, Jalili indicated provisional acceptance of the deal, along with an agreement to grant access to the newly public Iranian enrichment facility at Fordow—which the United States had known about for some time, but kept secret in order to suss out Iran's intent—and to meet again with technical experts later in October. Two weeks later, under the auspices of the IAEA, Iran, the United States, France, and Russia provisionally agreed to a TRR proposal (though some questions about how it would be orchestrated remained open and unresolved), sending it back to their respective governments for approval.

Quickly, it became clear that there was no political support in Tehran for the deal and that a renewed sanctions push might be necessary. At the end of October, anticipating a possible Iranian "no" answer, I led a small team to Brussels and Madrid to brief the EU and Spanish governments (which, at the time, served as the EU's president) on our sanctions work. We went through each of our sanctions ideas, laying the groundwork for future EU sanctions deliberations in anticipation that they would be needed but all the while hoping Iran would see the sense of the TRR deal.

Politics intervened in Tehran, involving even reform-minded politicians who opposed President Ahmadinejad's effort to cut a deal with the United States. Ahmadinejad had been badly damaged in Iranian politics with his disastrous reelection in June 2009, one marked with protests and widespread allegations of electoral fraud. Ahmadinejad did not have the ability to deliver Iran's agreement. In November 2009, President Obama authorized UN Ambassador Rice, Secretary Clinton, and Secretary Geithner to have their teams move forward with sanctions.

This took three forms, all of which proceeded together as part of an integrated, cohesive strategy: United Nations sanctions; informal multilateral measures; and U.S. domestic pressure on foreign corporations and banks.

First and foremost, there was the UN track. Though expectations for major UN sanctions were appropriately held in check, there was acknowledgment within the administration that the imprimatur of the UNSC would go a long way in convincing states to both implement the measures adopted by the UNSC (which, though a legal requirement, is far from assured in practice) and build upon those measures with national steps. Ambassador Rice and her team began working directly with their UN mission counterparts on the outlines of a sanctions resolution, drawing from ideas held since mid-2008's aborted attempt. Soon the interagency team was holding frequent videoconferences to develop concepts, back-up approaches, and notional language. The administration identified critical concepts, as well as "good to have" options. Our focus settled on four key elements, all of which found their way into resolution 1929, adopted on June 10, 2010.

PROVIDING A HOOK FOR FURTHER ENERGY SANCTIONS. It was clear from the start that the UNSC would not adopt specific, legally binding prohibitions on Iranian energy exports, even though the United States had identified them as a crucial pathway for creating sustained economic pressure on Iran due to Iran's reliance on oil exports for hard-currency earnings. We therefore asked our partners in Europe and Asia what they would need in order to push through their own national sanctions against Iranian energy supplies. We learned that preambular language in the resolution that identified Iran's energy sector as a problem would be sufficient. We crafted language that spoke to two elements of the notional threat: first, that Iran's energy sector provides Iran the wherewithal to evade the pressure of sanctions; and, second, that it could serve as a cover for Iran's procurement of nuclear and missile-related dual-use goods. The resulting UNSC language did just that:

> *Recognizing* that access to diverse, reliable energy is critical for sustainable growth and development, while noting the potential connection between Iran's revenues derived from its energy sector and the funding of Iran's proliferation-sensitive nuclear activities, and *further noting* that chemical process equipment and materials required for the petrochemical industry have much in common with those required for certain sensitive nuclear fuel cycle activities.[10]

CONTINUING TO TAR IRAN'S FINANCIAL SECTOR AS RIDDLED WITH ILLICIT ACTIVITY AND TO BE AVOIDED. Just as with the previous three resolutions imposing sanctions on Iran, the administration wanted to deepen Iran's financial isolation and make it easier for foreign governments to impose their own restrictions on Iran-related finance. This includes direct banking as well as export assistance, insurance, and all manner of finance-related services. The resulting UNSC resolution did that in multiple places in the main text and, crucially, also required the freezing of assets for one named Iranian bank—First East Export Bank—and the Iranian Revolutionary Guard Corps (IRGC) main legitimate business front, Khatam al-Anbia.

AUGMENTING UNSC AUTHORITIES FOR THE INSPECTION AND INTERDICTION OF CARGO. Even though states were permitted to inspect cargo and prevent the onward passage of sensitive goods to Iran from the start of the UNSC sanctions regime in 2006, many did not appreciate the sweep of their authorities. The administration prioritized giving states greater clarity about their ability to inspect, seize, and dispose of illicit cargo, ranging from sensitive nuclear and missile goods to conventional arms.

*INTENSIFYING THE EFFORT TO IDENTIFY AND REPORT VIOLA-
TIONS OF THE UNSC SANCTIONS REGIME.* The administration
sought and secured language in the resolution that provided for
the creation of a "Panel of Experts" to aid the UNSC and member states with the implementation of their obligations. This panel
soon became an invaluable part of the international community's
effort to track and identify for public awareness Iran's attempts
to evade sanctions, resulting in the formulation of guidance and
advice on best practices for states to use in their own implementation of the resolution. The panel's inspection reports of illicit
cargo identified and seized were particularly useful in stigmatizing
Iranian cargo shipments, particularly when entities and individuals affiliated with the IRGC were caught breaking the embargo in
West Africa in 2010.[11]

As noted, the UNSC track was not the only one of significance
in 2009–2010. The United States also sought to encourage national
measures by our partners, and we worked with Congress on a new
piece of U.S. sanctions legislation.

Partner sanctions were seen as a necessary, complementary element of UNSCR 1929 from the start. The United States worked
closely with the European Union, Japan, South Korea, Australia,
Canada, and others to develop sanctions options that would track
the measures included in the UN resolution and augment their
impact. Two particular elements stand out.

First, partners—particularly in the EU, Japan, and South Korea—
agreed to forgo investments in Iran's oil and gas sector, as well as
to withdraw any residual financial and technical support. Although
these governments did not prohibit the purchase of Iranian oil and
gas, this decision had two important, damaging effects on Iran: it
deprived the Iranian government of the resources needed to maintain, improve, and expand existing production facilities; and it
signaled that Iran's energy resources were legitimate, acceptable
targets for sanctions pressure. A concomitant U.S. announcement
that it would begin investigations under the Iran Sanctions Act of

companies involved in Iranian oil and gas investments helped to create impetus for this measure, as did a newly adopted "Special Rule" that would grant leniency for those entities that exited the Iranian market swiftly.[12]

Second, partners agreed to treat Iran's financial sector like a pariah, requiring preauthorization for a variety of transactions falling above certain financial thresholds (e.g., valued at over 40,000 euro) or involving certain parties. Iran's ability to engage in normal business was compromised as a result. But, perhaps more important, the sense of normalcy around Iran's economy was badly damaged. Iran was seen as being "special," and not in a good way. Iran business would be complex, difficult to manage, and potentially costly. The result was that, although some large companies persevered and some small companies took the risk, there was a flood of institutions out of Iran in 2010.

The U.S. sanctions legislation accelerated this exodus. In June 2010, just after the UNSCR was adopted, President Obama signed into law the Comprehensive Iran Sanctions, Accountability, and Divestment Act (CISADA). CISADA was comprised of many different forms of sanctions measures, some of which intensified existing U.S. sanctions on oil and gas investment in Iran or the penalties associated with breach of the U.S. sanctions regime. But by far the most important provision of CISADA was to be found in Section 104, which created the basis for essentially a financial embargo of Iran. In this provision—which had been negotiated laboriously by executive branch and legislative branch representatives starting in 2009—the United States acquired the power to turn off foreign bank access to the United States if those foreign banks were found to be processing transactions either for U.S.-designated Iranian financial institutions or the IRGC. With the expansion of the U.S. designation list of Iranian banks, the international financial system found that any transaction with Iran risked the possibility of losing access to the United States. Even though some financial institutions without a U.S. link might survive such a sanction with little difficulty, multinational banks feared this provision and joined the rush of entities abandoning business with Iran. The plain truth was that Iran was a lucrative market, but the United States was more so. It simply made no economic sense to risk U.S. access for the opportunities that existed in Iran.

These three levels of sanctions—UN, multinational, and corporate (enforced by U.S. coercion)—hammered Iran from a variety of different angles starting in June 2010 with UNSCR 1929's adoption. By the end of the summer of 2010, Iran faced similar bad news nearly every week, with U.S., EU, Japanese, Korean, Australian, and Canadian legislation all being adopted and enforced. The pressure was intense, unrelenting, and sustained. Unfortunately, it did not generate any meaningful Iranian negotiation concessions, despite being increased steadily over the next two years.

6

On Target Response and Resolve

IN CHAPTER 4, I categorized sanctions. I also discussed how to assign value to the pain of sanctions and how to ensure that pain registers as anticipated and desired. In chapter 5, we saw the application of this effort with respect to Iran from 2006 through 2010. In this chapter, I discuss the response of sanctioned countries, entities, and individuals as a general matter. As I outlined in chapter 1, the degree to which the targeted state intends to persevere with its original activity notwithstanding the imposition of pain by the sanctioner is what we will define as its national "resolve." A primary component of resolve is how important the subject of sanctions is relative to other national priorities.

First, we must consider how states organize themselves around national priorities. Countries have bands of priorities, in which some things are weighed as more important than others, depending on the national character, history, government structure, societal makeup and needs of the population. Again, although exhaustive research can probably articulate this point with more precision, the inference is logical: more abstract priorities tend to be set aside when issues of national survival are at stake. For this reason, countries in crisis tend to have national debates, seeking to evaluate whether the situation justifies changes to underlying priorities or if staying the course is best. The United States, for example, has struggled since 9/11 with the conflict between safety and security on the one hand and personal liberties on the other. Other countries have similarly experienced the pull of one priority or another in certain circumstances.

Countries probably value some interests more than others consistently over time. Individuals may change their viewpoints on which interest is most important at any given moment, but systems and governments establish notional—if unwritten—rules for how they prioritize their interests. Territorial integrity, for instance, is a common top-shelf priority for states. It is a reason why most states have standing armies or navies, with infrastructure to support their employment in exigent circumstances. For some states, however, the separation between the importance of territorial integrity and another interest—say, economic performance—may be wider or narrower. In Europe, members of the European Union's Schengen Zone have implicitly decided that one element of territorial integrity—controlling transit through national borders—is less important than the economic costs of delayed travel. Several European states have also determined that a common currency is of sufficient value as to sacrifice national control over the currency used in their territories (just as some countries, in accepting the use of the U.S. dollar instead of their own national currencies, have elected to cede control over their monetary policy in order to harvest the benefits of being aligned with the dollar).

Priorities can change over time coincident with broader developments that change previous convictions and beliefs. Priorities can also flip due to internal or external factors. For example, countries in the EU have witnessed the limitations that a common currency places on their ability to use monetary policy to address economic problems since the 2009 Great Recession.

This has even resulted in consideration among some—Greece most prominently—to reverse their previous willingness to cede national control, even if the original rationale for coming together to form the euro remains fully intact.

Just as priorities have national bases and must be considered from within that analytical framework, so too must sanctioners reevaluate their understanding of those priorities to ensure that their understanding remains current. Saddam Hussein's willingness to sacrifice the interests of his subjects in order to advance his own peculiar notions of national interest is well established. It is reasonable to assume that no amount of sanctions pain would have been able to overwhelm Saddam's desire to advance Iraqi national sovereignty, which—as he saw it—was incompatible with intrusive international inspections of suspect military sites. In the end, this extended to a readiness to accept military force employed against him, despite the fact that only twelve years earlier, the same military forces had routed his military, then the world's fourth largest.

As noted in chapter 2, observers have speculated as to why this is. But the most logical conclusion is that he believed such intrusion would badly puncture his sense of (and perhaps actual) deterrence for regional adversaries and, domestically, potential rivals. Or he may have simply miscalculated. Either way, his acceptance of invasion before acceptance of uninhibited inspections forms a picture as to his interests and priorities. This picture puts resisting cooperation with the international community well above his interest in preserving the territorial integrity of Iraq, the Iraqi economy, the well-being of the Iraqi population, and Iraq's standing in the international community.

It is unlikely that Saddam Hussein's resolve was equal for each factor over time. Far more likely is that he did begin with a preference to observe all of his national priorities, but that with a decade of sanctions, some lost their importance. For example, even though Saddam played games with international inspectors for over ten years, as of 2002, it appears he was prepared to accept at least limited cooperation with the international community, evidenced by the return of UN inspectors to the country in 2002. Iraq's readiness to offer limited cooperation to inspectors toward the end of 2002 but failure to extend this cooperation to the full access demanded by the United States, United Kingdom, and their partners suggests that coalition pressure was sufficient to have crossed the "deny limited cooperation" priority threshold but was insufficient to coerce Iraq into offering full cooperation and far from capable of forcing Saddam to voluntarily relinquish power.

Divining priorities starts, naturally, with an understanding of the country itself, as suggested in chapter 4. But identifying a more explicit sense of prioritization to create an effective sanctions regime requires more. Documents and publicly available materials can be helpful, such as the following (which will be examined in further detail later on in this chapter):

- Budget allocations
- Political platforms or manifestos
- Constitutional requirements
- Popular views/concerns
- National strategy documents and speeches

For some countries, however, the picture may be contained in a more complete understanding of the workings of the regime. For example, in North Korea's case, one could argue that an unstated but central priority for the elites in power is the dominance of the Kim family and the Communist Party. For Iran, one could identify maintaining the present theocratic government as a significant priority, something that might not be identified by name in any of these documents. But at the same time, expert analysts of a country's policies, politics, and society can help to identify what those priorities are and how to rank them in the grand scheme of things.

Priorities also have some constituent parts. One could break apart any individual line of national interest to identify specific sub-priorities and shading for them. For example, "territorial integrity" could be defined in terms of control of all borders—as is a priority for the United States—or in more geostrategic terms, as many European countries have established in their willingness to open internal borders while at the same time affirming their participation in NATO and other security-focused organizations. Likewise, "economy" as a priority can be subject to many differentiations, with priority attached to growth rates, inflation rates, unemployment rates, or even individual economic sectors.

Coercive diplomacy and the strategy of sanctions seek to exploit the multiplicity of interests by pitting one set of interests against another for a country. The bargain being offered to a sanctions target is continued application of pain or its relaxation in response to concessions by the target, with the severity of pain required dependent on the nature of the interest. Or, put another way, the sanctioner is trying to seek the right decision on a choice the target would not have otherwise made.

The key point of sanctions leverage, therefore, lies in targeting accurately the resolve threshold that you wish to crack and developing a usable estimate of how much pain and pressure is required to cross it. For example, one could threaten the territorial integrity of a country—which may be accorded a higher status of resolve and therefore interest—in order to achieve a change of position on a lower resolve threshold item. In other cases, it may be possible to incentivize a change in behavior on a lower-level interest in exchange for benefits for a higher-level interest. For example, offering economic benefits to a country might encourage it to make changes to its nuclear program, while threatening its territorial integrity could compel it to do the same.

If we assume that resolve is variable based on the interests in question, then it follows that resolve also does not hold to a set level across time. It can and will change depending on circumstances, and of course that is a core objective of sanctions. But some aspects of resolve may not change. For example, it is plausible to conjecture that territorial integrity may be uniformly important over time, but diplomatic reputation might change as pain is applied. Or one could even suggest that territorial integrity could—in time—become something worth sacrificing in order to preserve economic prosperity, if the sacrifice were comparatively small in exchange with the benefits to be accrued (say, trading an island to keep the peace). This certainly has been done in the past, as territory was frequently swapped among European powers both before and during the period of colonization; in fact, China's willingness to cede control of Hong Kong to the United Kingdom in the 1800s in response to a military threat is a demonstration of the variable nature of priorities at certain times and in response to certain stimuli. One would be hard put to imagine the same sort of decision being made by the current government of China or being demanded, for that matter, by the current government of the United Kingdom which, unlike China, has largely maintained a consistent system of government throughout the intervening decades.

Target Response

Responses to sanctions by those targeted can run the gamut but are thought to fall into two broad baskets: sanctions can be accepted and their impacts managed, or sanctions can be rejected and actively resisted.

As far as sanctions "acceptance" is concerned, I do not intend to connote "welcomed." This chapter (and, indeed, the entire theory of coercive diplomacy) proceeds from the assumption that sanctions-induced pain is something its targets wish to avoid. This is not to say that targets cannot make the best of a bad situation and embrace the consequences of sanctions, possibly to their advantage, as will be examined shortly. This surely happens and is part of a target's response to sanctions. But we discount the circumstances—or hypothetical conjectures—in which a sanctions target specifically sought or may seek to be subject to sanctions. As noted in chapter 1, there could be many reasons for such a decision—including to seek an upper hand in internal political disputes or for individual actors to take advantage of their own commercial opportunities under sanctions—but, for purposes of this chapter, we'll assume that the imposition of sanctions and the pain that comes along with them is not desirable.

Instead, "acceptance" is intended to connote acknowledgment, but with a heavy sigh. Those that fall into this group of sanctions targets do not necessarily change their modus operandi or bend to the will of the sanctioning state. But neither do they attempt to challenge the imposition of sanctions or avoid the consequences that result. Instead, they adapt themselves to the imposition of sanctions and then identify ways of either profiting from the experience or using it for political gain (either domestically for regime cohesion or internationally to generate sympathy). Venezuela's reaction to the imposition of U.S. sanctions against seven of its officials in 2015 can be seen as a demonstration of this latter approach, as Venezuela was able to appeal to international partners to rebuff another example of Yankee imperialism and beleaguered Venezuelan president Nicolás Maduro even experienced a bump in his polling numbers.[1]

Rejection and resistance to sanctions is the more traditional, expected response. In this approach, targets instead seek to find ways around the sanctions, either through clandestine smuggling or by establishing economic ties with states, companies, or individuals prepared to court the risk of their own punishment. This response can also be accompanied by retaliatory sanctions, as when Russia imposed agriculture bans against the EU in 2014 in response to economic sanctions imposed over Russia's interference in the sovereignty of Ukraine. The overall approach is to try to minimize the negative impact of the sanctions by outflanking them or to seek to level similar pain on the original sanctioner and its interests.

Iran offers another real-life illustration of this hypothetical. In 2009–2010, the conventional wisdom in Washington was that the imposition of sanctions on Iran's import of gasoline and other petroleum products would bring the Iranian government to its knees. Then-representative of Illinois Mark Kirk (a vocal proponent of sanctions against Iran) argued in 2010 that a gasoline quarantine would have such dire consequences that it would force Iran to concede on its nuclear program and other illicit activities.[2] A sanction on Iran's import of gasoline was duly included in CISADA, which—as outlined in the preceding chapter—became law in July 2010. What happened? Rather than Iran collapsing or immediately conceding on any of these various illicit activities, the country instead applied itself to a combination of smuggling and transformation of its existing petrochemical plants for gasoline production to meet its domestic needs. The result has been gasoline that observers have blamed for the increase in environmental pollution in Iran. Still, Iran has managed to keep cars on the road. The failure in this example was not that of sanctions enforcement per se: Iranian importation of gasoline duly dropped from an annual average of 132,100 barrels per day in 2009 to 39,600 barrels per day in 2011.[3] Rather, the failure was in not appreciating the importance that Iran would place on keeping cars on the road and its ability to undertake unconventional means to solve the problems created by sanctions. In other words, Iran felt the pain being inflicted via a gasoline ban as manageable rather than a knock-out blow. For the ban's proponents, the failure of this strategy was taken as a sign of Iranian stubbornness (which, to some extent, is probably right) and—worse—ill intent in terms of the nuclear program. But even when concluding that more sanctions pressure was needed, it is important to consider that the failure of the gasoline ban might not have stemmed from Iranian intransigence but instead from the selection of pain its recipient—in the end—was able to reject.

The intention behind both rejection and resistance is to deflect the impact on target decision making. While the pain may still exist, its psychological impact may therefore be neutered. Resolve is, after all, a function of complex psychological and physically tangible variable interactions. It results from estimates of one's own tolerance for pain in the future, the likelihood of increasing pain, the coherence of that pain, and its intensity. With strategies to protect resolve, those targeted by sanctions both up the ante with their adversaries and reinforce their own positions.

Measuring Resolve

Just as with pain, resolve can also be measured based on knowledge of a sanctions target. As shown already, if the national interest value is higher for a particular activity, it may be more impervious to change via the application of pain from sanctions, but this does not necessarily equate with being unswerving. The critical factor is the nature of the pain applied.

Measuring these changes, however, is more abstract and subject to complex internal dynamics than those directly associated with sanctions pain, which can be measured externally and—to some degree—objectively. A simple illustration can help make this point. Let us assume that mild sanctions are imposed on a state for a particular bad act. However, let us also assume that the country being sanctioned was in the midst of an election cycle, with those vying for leadership seeking to demonstrate that they are "tougher" than the other in resisting the outside world. The resulting statements of resolve to weather sanctions may give a variety of false impressions to the sanctioner that ultimately could lead the sanctioning state either to intensify sanctions again—contributing to an escalatory cycle—or to abandon them as not worth the risk of said escalation.

Either way, there is tremendous uncertainty in the measurement of sanctions effect on national resolve. In the absence of clear countervailing information, parties in the sanctioning jurisdiction fall back on their individual biases and assumptions. If you believe your sanctions are working, you'll dismiss the tough talk and focus on the economics. If you don't, you will buy the tough talk and assume either that sanctions need strengthening (if a sanctions hawk) or that they are having a counterproductive effect. In other words, even though the people imposing sanctions had some reasonable ways of estimating how much pressure was being applied, they may have greater difficulty in understanding how this pressure might shift the commitment of the sanctioned party from its desired course of action.

The most effective way to handle this confusion is to develop a set of potential indicators so that an overall understanding of the trend can be developed. Once developed, they should be checked frequently during sanctions imposition to establish whether they indicate progress being made or sanctions pressure being lost. There are a number of potential indictors, the value of which will depend greatly on the nature of the country being sanctioned, the nature of its economy, and the nature of any domestic pressure feedback loops for the leadership of that country. Items of particular interest include the following:

- Public statements by government officials
- Propaganda levels and focus
- Economic indicators (particularly those indicating growth and sustained performance in the face of sanctions)
- Internal political developments
- Polling data on popular sentiments and regime support
- Positions taken in negotiations and international fora

Let us look at each of these in greater depth to consider the range of possibilities and their meanings.

Public Statements by Government Officials

Public statements are problematic as a means of measuring national resolve because they are intended, by and large, to serve as a demonstration of resolve. Of course, if an official statement indicates that an issue is no longer of the same significance or that the country is prepared to back down, then it is relatively easy to use such statements as a means by which resolve can be measured.

Unfortunately, adversaries rarely make life that easy for one another. Even if total capitulation is on offer by a sanctioned jurisdiction, national pride would likely inhibit bold expressions of resignation. Instead, public statements from threatened parties are often meant to deny any indication of weakness. Not for nothing was former Iraqi information minister Muhammad Saeed al-Sahhaf ridiculed during the 2003 invasion of his country for his bold proclamations of total victory for Iraqi troops while Western media reported U.S. tanks were on the outskirts of Baghdad. Less extravagant examples could also be conjured but tell the same tale of government officials seeking to influence rather than inform their audiences, much less to inform adversaries seeking to inflict pain.

Yet, at the same time, government statements can be telling, and experts on a particular topic or country's policies may still be able to intuit what is intended. Removing the outlier of Sahhaf, there is a wide array of potentially believable government spokespeople who are forced to manage real problems in their defense of national policy. Iranian spokespeople, for example, have long sought to tread a very narrow line between blaming the United States and its partners for its economic problems while at the same time sustaining the official line that sanctions pressure is at worst meaningless and at best salutary for indigenous Iranian economic development. In their statements, one can detect this thread and see that, over time, the pressure brought by economic sanctions was making life steadily more difficult for the Iranian government and changing the messaging. To illustrate this point, we can examine the statements by the Iranian representative to the IMF-World Bank Group Annual Meetings (located on the IMF's website). From 2007 to 2008, these statements suggested that Iran was irritated but not yet uncomfortable, using figures and data to illustrate the point. From 2009 to 2012, these statements suggested that Iran saw the forum as a place to lodge complaints about the pernicious impact of sanctions while avoiding getting into specifics. From 2013 to 2014 (as we shall see), these statements suggested that the new Rouhani government sought to change the tone. The Rouhani approach shifted again in 2014 with the Iranian government choosing to speak about figures again, likely because the numbers were more attractive.

How to separate the wheat from the chaff is the province of country experts, who can offer advice on the subtle uses of language and shifts in presentation. But some key markers include:

THE SIMPLE ACT OF ACKNOWLEDGMENT. Acknowledging that you have a sanctions problem is half the battle for those under outside pressure. It is difficult for governments to admit this truth, in part because it underscores to the adversary that the vulnerability it was seeking to exploit was in fact exploitable. Not for nothing has there been a history of such statements being characterized as "sowing fear and despondency" within a population. But such acknowledgment also serves an important function for sanctioned jurisdictions: they can appeal to nationalism within the country and gain points for having admitted what may be painfully obvious rather than pretending such pressure did not and does not exist. Either way, a simple acknowledgment of the reality of sanctions pressure is an indication that the pressure is starting to bite.

APPEALS TO NATIONALISM AND RESILIENCY. Although simple acknowledgment is the first signal, a direct appeal to citizens to resist the pressure being applied is an important indicator as well. Calls for resistance are not limited to those under sanctions, but the reframing of sanctions pressure into "economic warfare" by the target is indicative of a sanctions campaign that is starting to have a toll. The use of religious references may also reinforce the value of this shift from the perspective of interpretation, but it depends on the nature of religion in the given society.

USE OF DIFFERENT LANGUAGES FOR INTERNAL AND EXTERNAL MESSAGING. An indicator worth noting is the language in which messages are conveyed. Use of English in a nonnative English speaking country, for example, could underscore that the message is meant for external consumption, speaking either to foreign investors or foreign governments depending on the message. Likewise, mixed or ambiguous translations—or disputed translations after the fact—might also point to an attempt by a sanctioned state to avoid the problematic implications of the message being conveyed.

Propaganda Levels and Focus

Somewhat distinct from official statements of the sort outlined above is the matter of government propaganda. Propaganda can serve a useful informative role for measuring resolve, particularly the kinds of messages that are being pushed.

For our purposes, we will define "propaganda" as the system of government-sponsored messages that are not identifiable with any particular personality or spokesperson, but rather those that radiate out into the environment through radio or television placement, billboards, paper flyers, and similar means.

Messages will vary depending on the national economic and political systems, as well as the prevailing culture. But key sign-posts may be appeals to:

- thrift and reduced luxury purchases, particularly from for-eign sources (to lower import bills)
- revitalize domestic industrial bases and the development of new, indigenous industry
- rally around the flag, treating present economic circum-stances as economic warfare meriting solidarity and unity; and
- identify and report instances of public corruption.

The sum total of these messages is that the country is under strain and that citizens can help mitigate it. The first indication of a problem is the creation of targeted propaganda itself; its intensi-fication and shifting messages over time can serve as a demonstra-tion of deepening appreciation of the problem—demonstrating the overall impact of sanctions pressure and helping with its mea-surement—as well as national resolve if these messages look to pin blame on particular groups or divert attention away from the underlying problem.

More subtly, the intensification of propaganda over time can be a signpost of wavering resolve, particularly if the message begins to shift. Take, for example, messages from the Iranian government to its population about the significance of specific nuclear projects from 2003 to 2013. They were symbols of potent significance in their own right, with inaugural activities hosted at multiple times. By the end of 2016, the messages from the government were different, emphasizing the overall progress of the Iranian nation and its development of advanced technologies and capabilities. Specific facilities or projects are less important in this vein than the overall trend line, which makes sense given that the Iranian government gave up considerable capacities—for at least for ten to fifteen years—in the JCPOA. Seen from the out-side, one could argue that this signpost emerged as negotiations began, helping some within the Iranian government to redefine the debate and condition the population for concessions to come. In other words, what was arguably a demonstration of resolve and strength actually became a way of signaling that the Iranian government was preparing to make concessions and that its resolve to maintain those present projects was weakening.

In Iraq, government propaganda was far more personal, aimed at burnishing the image of Saddam Hussein and the strength of the Iraqi army in managing the threats coming from the outside world. He sought to suppress information that could undermine his public stance of unshakable, immutable defiance and held that to the last.

Economic Indicators

Economic indicators are the most straightforward markers of national resolve to obtain, but potentially as difficult to interpret as public statements or propaganda. One can readily develop pictures of economic health for most countries under sanctions (with North Korea an exception that may even prove the rule, given that the difficulty of the task has hardly stopped people from making the attempt). Moreover, the pictures developed can receive some degree of corroboration from external sources. Trade data, for example, can be gathered both from the sanctioned state and from its trading partners, allowing for a stronger interpretation and more confidence in what the data gathered might mean. Even other data streams that rely on purely domestic collection can be subjected to verification. Unemployment and inflation data can be manipulated by a government, but the person on the street can tell an observer whether he or she has a job, for how many hours a week, and what the price of chicken is at the local butcher. Official statistics can also be scrutinized by the sanctioned country's own population, which—to varying degrees depend on the freedom of speech laws and practices at home—can be aired publicly.

The difficulty comes in ascertaining what the statistics mean in terms of national resolve. For example, a 5 percent contraction in GDP is a significant economic event. But how that contraction is felt matters in terms of how effective the sanction is; so too does the overall starting size of the economy and where the loss is felt directly. Likewise, unemployment climbing above 40 percent is a sign of economic illness, but perhaps less so in a country where 20 percent unemployment has been endemic for a generation. Inflation figures can also be subject to the same interpretative endeavor.

In other words, as has been stressed throughout this book, the important part in interpreting the effect of economic indicators on national resolve is to avoid facile comparisons or non-context-specific generalizations. Indicators of poor economic performance matter in some places more than others, meaning that the temptation to mirror image the reaction to economic problems in one place to one's own experience needs to be checked. Measuring the impact of sanctions, as noted above, needs to be in relation to the status quo, not the ideal, and measuring national resolve merits the same consideration.

Of course, there is also the possibility that economic indicators are of such sensitivity for a country that it refuses to release them or—in the case of Iraq in the 1990s—classifies them as sensitive national security information.[4] This, in and of itself, can also constitute a source of information of both the nature of the statistic being obscured and the fear of the country in question. Iran, by contrast, continued publishing economic statistics throughout the 2006–2013 sanctions campaign, but it is believed to have tinkered with them in order to present a less negative image.[5] Official statistics of Iranian unemployment, for example, downplayed significantly the absolute number of unemployed Iranians as well as the level of inflation throughout the country. That said, some statistics are hard to obscure. For example, even though Iran maintained an official exchange rate with the U.S. dollar throughout the sanctions period, it resisted attempts to reconcile this rate with the black-market rate, which at some points was up to three times higher than the official rate. Likewise, attempts to distort the inflation figure were belied by people being able to go into the market place and simply do the math on how much more consumer goods cost on one day versus the previous day. The same sort of math undermined Iraq's attempt to maintain an official fiction as to the state of the overall economy.

For sanctioners, even distorted statistics have some value. If badly distorted, then they highlight the degree to which economic performance is a vulnerability and—depending on what factor is distorted—a potentially acute pressure point. For Iran, sanctioners observed that unemployment and underemployment were sensitivities; therefore, sanctioners sought to exacerbate the problem. The same applied to the weakness of the Iranian currency, dependent as it was on the supply of hard currency from exports abroad. It became an integral part of the strategy to undermine perception of the strength of the Iranian rial by the population as well as to dilute the currency itself by depriving Iran of the hard currency it needed.

Internal Political Developments

This indicator may be, on the surface, less applicable to autocracies than democracies. But all governments have politics; indeed, all organizations have politics, as anyone who has ever worked in a group larger than two people can testify.

Kim Jong Un of North Korea may be a prototypical autocrat whose personal and national interests are fully distinct from the interests of his people. Arguably, nuclear weapons possession is only of value to Kim and his ruling clique, as it permits them greater protection from outside interference (though the devastation that could be wrought in a Korean peninsular war today, even without nuclear weapons, is surely also a deterrent). For the people of North Korea, their leadership may argue that nuclear weapons protect them, but considering their greatest enemy is their own government, outside threats are hardly their biggest problem.

For Kim, it is arguable that almost no level of economic pressure would be sufficient to topple him, at least given current views of the consolidated nature of his regime. Assuming that he can maintain control of his inner circle through a combination of perks and threats, Kim is largely in a position to sustain his authority. He is fully prepared to pass on the effects of any pressure to his population, and they are essentially powerless to affect him in turn. Moreover, as a result of the country's economic insularity, there are few sectors against which pressure could be applied (though, as we shall see in chapter 9, that doesn't mean an effort cannot be made to find sources of leverage).

In contrast, fully functional democracies are highly vulnerable to domestic political pressure created by sanctions. Take, for example, the boycott, divestment, and sanctions (BDS) campaign against Israel in response to concerns about the stalemated nature of Palestinian-Israeli peace talks and Israeli treatment of the Palestinians in the interim. To an open economy and democratic society like Israel's, BDS is a real threat not only to the growth potential of the country but also to its diplomatic relations with the rest of the world, its integration into the Western world and its culture, and the political stability of its government. Some Israelis are rightly frustrated with their treatment under the BDS campaign (though others have even gone to court to protect their right to campaign *in favor* of BDS). Regardless, there is an ongoing debate as to the underlying causes of the campaign and who is to blame for its intensification over the last several years. There is also ongoing disagreement about the costs of BDS, with some questioning its effectiveness and others—including the RAND Corporation, with a fascinating online calculator—estimating that Israel could stand to lose approximately $47 billion over ten years due to BDS and related problems.[6] What this internal turmoil prompts as a response is another matter, but for purposes of this study, the interesting facet is that the debate is being had and pressure is being created on the Israeli government to deal with the problem.[7] Such pressure would likely not be felt (or would be felt less) if the Israeli government was not a democracy with a free market economy.

Of course, what is happening inside of one type of government may be more visible than in another. For democracies, the political developments are somewhat more transparent. Ministers can be sacked for failure to manage situations that lead to the imposition of sanctions or have their responsibilities realigned. Ultimately, even a country's head of government could be replaced as a consequence of the imposition of sanctions and/or the failure to manage the situation effectively.

Autocracies also have their political currents, albeit in ways that may be peculiar to observe and inscrutable to outsiders. During the Cold War, intelligence analysts and newspaper reporters alike sought to understand who was in power and who was not in the Soviet Union by engaging in Kremlinology, often by taking note of who was standing closest to the Soviet premier in photographs. The same sorts of practices can be used in evaluating the political undercurrents of other countries.

But to what end? Internal political developments are not just interesting from a country-level perspective. They are also potentially indicative of real shifts of power and influence in a country. In this way, they can also point to changes in regime perspective on particular issues or the degree to which a national priority has become an essential interest. Of course, these signals can also be misinterpreted. In 2009, the head of the Atomic Energy Organization of Iran (AEOI), Reza Aghazadeh, was replaced by Ali Salehi. Some observers saw this as a potentially welcome shift of Iranian perspective on the nuclear program, with Salehi being seen by some as a deal-making, Western-thinking pragmatist in comparison with Aghazadeh. Yet, five years later during negotiations over the JCPOA, Salehi—reprising this role after a stint as Iran's foreign minister—was often quoted as drawing tough lines for nuclear negotiators to manage. One way of interpreting this apparent shift is that Aghazadeh's removal was not a signal to the West, but rather an attempt by the Iranian government to replace a less competent manager of the nuclear program with a better one; in other words, Salehi's appointment underscored the *importance* of the nuclear program, not the beginning of a more accommodating phase in the Iranian nuclear program. In fact, the number of centrifuges installed from Salehi's initial appointment in 2009 until January 2011 doubled.[8]

For this reason, like all other measures, it is not prudent to consider domestic political developments as independently important variables, because their meaning can be misinterpreted. Rather, they should be seen as important elements of a larger picture. For example, while Salehi's appointment in 2009 may not have been indicative of a mindset shift, the election of Hassan Rouhani to the presidency in June 2013 (and on a platform of rebuilding the Iranian economy through a more positive interaction with the outside world) did mark a real transition in the approach of the Iranian government to one that is both more interested in foreign perspectives and willing to accommodate foreign concerns with its nuclear program. His election marked the end of a period of intense sanctions escalation against Iran, and his campaign focused on the imperative of removing international sanctions as a means of achieving economic growth. The political development of Rouhani being elected and permitted to become president of Iran (considering that the Iranian political system is designed to weed out those who are deemed inappropriate) could be interpreted as an indication of weakening Iranian resolve to stand against international concerns and readiness to take another approach.

Polling Data on Popular Sentiments
and Regime Support

This takes us to the issue of polling data and similar expressions of popular sentiments. As with internal political dynamics, this indicator is probably more easily observed in democratic systems of government than in autocracies. Yet, even in most autocracies, there are ways to measure and assess the views of the population, including through polling. Certainly, polls in authoritarian jurisdictions merit some degree of skepticism unless their methodologies sufficiently exclude the possibility of knee-jerk support for government policies, whatever they may be. But to the degree that polling can confidently describe national priorities and interests, they can be useful in helping to develop a picture of the target country's perspectives. And, importantly, they can be used to identify which issues might be sufficient cause to provoke civil unrest or, at a minimum, civil discontent.

Polls from Saddam's Iraq are difficult to find. Official election results from Iraq routinely placed Saddam above 99 percent in his "reelection" campaigns.[9] In Iran, by contrast, there has been a steady accumulation of polls during the course of the 1990s and 2000s, helping to inform outsiders on the nature and evolution of Iranian public thinking. For example, prior to 2005, the nuclear program did not rate very highly in importance for Iranians.[10] After the 2005–2013 sanctions, when the nuclear program was daily news, polling reflects increased interest in and attachment to the program.[11] Likewise, polling data changed over time with respect to public sentiments on the threat of sanctions to the Iranian economy and the importance of removing those sanctions in a deal.[12] That said, polling in an authoritarian system like Iran comes with its own challenges, beyond those that afflict polling everywhere (e.g., with respect to finding an appropriate sample size, dealing with outlier opinions, and the fickle nature of respondents). Polling is therefore useful to add data for consideration by policy makers, but may not be determinative.

Positions Taken in Negotiations and International Fora

Last, one can take a country's representatives at their word when they describe national interests during the course of negotiations. There are ample opportunities for representatives of governments to lay out their perspectives, concerns, and priorities in a range of negotiating and other international fora from the United Nations to specialized international agencies to unofficial workshops. Statements of position in these places may not differ markedly from what officials are prepared to enter onto the record in more public statements. But, in some cases, they can offer glimpses into the calculations made by all governments when assessing problems.

Certainly, this is the case in negotiations themselves. Once negotiations move beyond anodyne statements of position, they usually involve an exchange of views on how particular issues might be solved that expose the nature of the interests involved. Sometimes, these statements can shift, creating confusion, but oftentimes there is broad consistency between public and private positioning.

Where Does This Leave Us?

Identifying ways to measure and evaluate pain and resolve conditions is useful, but it falls short without some kind of construct into which they can be placed. Worse, the fact that indicators could all point in different directions runs the risk that, far from being a way of understanding better the design and impact of sanctions, considerations of pain and resolve could become just tools for justifying or criticizing in hindsight the decisions made by policymakers.

To some extent, these are unavoidable risks. Foreign policy inherently deals with imprecision in national positions and perspectives, made more indistinct by the real benefits countries can sometimes garner from having their positions misunderstood by their adversary. But there are also problems inherent in deliberately sowing misunderstanding. This book proceeds from the notion that, for all of the incentive to mislead and distort positions, states naturally incline toward conveying some semblance of the truth in their official pronouncements and perspectives. If a state says that it claims sovereignty over a jurisdiction and will refuse to relinquish it, then it is folly to enter the conversation with an assumption that this is altogether untrue. Rather, what's more sensible is to assume that the position being expressed is—at a minimum—a going-in position meriting serious attention but potentially subject to revision. Though a state can modify its positions over time, such initial positioning should be taken as, if not the ideal outcome, a desired outcome.

From these assumptions, it is possible to instead use information about sanctions justifications, the measures themselves, and the perspectives of the sanctioned state to give an adequate, if rough, approximation of relative interests, willingness to apply economic force, and willingness to resist it.

7

Intense Pressure on Iran and a Turn to Real Negotiations

IN CHAPTER 5, I went through the escalation of sanctions pressure from 2006 to 2010. I noted that, though pressure was intensifying, Iran's response was far from constructive by the end of 2010. Yet, only three years later, an agreement had been fashioned by the P5+1 (composed of China, France, Germany, Russia, the United Kingdom, and the United States, under the coordination of the European Union) and Iran that not only deescalated the situation but also set a path for the comprehensive agreement of 2015.

Both intensified pain and intensified resolve are part of this story. But in the end, the pain that was applied by the P5+1 (and the United States, in particular) overwhelmed Iran's ability to resist sanctions and created the need to come to a negotiated settlement.

Intensifying Pressure

As described in chapter 5, the United States employed a three-part sanctions strategy starting in 2010, combining implementation of multinational measures at both the UN and national levels with its own coercive national measures. We then spent the bulk of 2010 and 2011 urging states to implement fully the measures that they already had in place.

This was harder than it sounds. For one thing, there are fundamental capacity issues that plague most bureaucracies with respect to sanctions. They are labor intensive, requiring intelligence collection, information analysis, and investigation. They are politically sensitive, requiring in some cases decisions about whether to continue with business, personal contacts, and diplomatic relationships that domestic constituencies support and foreign powers oppose. And last but not least, they are potentially economically fraught, requiring a decision to forgo profitable lines of business in order to achieve a result that may be uncertain and may not even be all that important to the state in question.

Iran involved all three forms of difficulty. For one thing, Iran's strategy of sanctions resistance involved sophisticated—if occasionally straightforward—evasion efforts. Iran's clandestine procurement agents established front companies around the world, often in jurisdictions with weak national legislation governing their behavior. Iran's financiers likewise exploited vulnerabilities in financial-sector monitoring and enforcement to create conduits for the flow of payments and hard currency that otherwise would have been prohibited. The United States was in a position to help foreign governments deal with some of these challenges, but not all of them; after all, the U.S. capacity is also not limitless, and the number of sanctions enforcement priorities that existed from 2010 to 2013 at times swamped enforcement officers. Likewise, intelligence resources are finite and subject to restraints on their use, particularly if the intent is to pass along sensitive information to foreign governments. Even in cases where the United States might have wanted to intervene to strengthen a foreign investigation, there were limits on what we could do to prompt foreign action and how we could respond to requests for assistance. Consequently, many observers and some of my own colleagues likened U.S. efforts to an elaborate, never-ending game of "whack-a-mole" (though I often remarked while in government that I usually win at that game during my family's annual sojourn to Hershey Park, Pennsylvania).

Moreover although many Americans find this difficult to conceive, Iran is not seen around the world as a categorically unhelpful or unpleasant actor. Many states—particularly those in the Non-Aligned Movement, a group of states organized during the Cold War that sought to avoid becoming entangled in U.S.-Soviet bloc competition and which found new life in the 1990s as a device to assert the interests of the developing world—are broadly supportive of many of Iran's positions, particularly with respect to its nuclear program. These states and even some states that are part of the U.S. alliance structure do not necessarily see Iran or its policies as threatening. Consequently, the United States needed to develop an organizing principle for multinational action, one that all participants could support. Of course, the engagement approach undertaken by President Obama was part and parcel of this effort, as was the Bush-era attempt to demonstrate that Iran's nuclear program was developed in secret, contrary to Iran's international nonproliferation obligations. The Obama administration took these pillars of U.S. diplomatic strategy and augmented them with a simple, but powerful, argument: failure to resolve the Iranian nuclear issue diplomatically would increase the chances of another war in the Middle East, something few if any members of the international community wished to see. Obama underscored this risk by stating, clearly, that he was prepared to use force to prevent Iran from acquiring a nuclear weapon, although it was not his preferred outcome.[1]

Ironically, Iran's own belligerent posture—particularly in December 2011 through January 2012—may have helped demonstrate the risks and the need to cooperate with U.S. sanctions.

In late December, Iranian officials made statements that indicated willingness to close the Straits of Hormuz, a vital waterway for the entire Persian Gulf. U.S. military representatives in the Persian Gulf restated the long-standing U.S. position that no state would be permitted to impede free navigation of the Straits, leading to a war of words between Iran and the United States over the next few weeks. Tensions eventually subsided, in part because of a reduction of Iranian saber rattling. Though unprovable, it seems likely that messages and delegations to and from important states outside of the region (notably China) may have impressed upon Iran the need to back down. Regardless, and coincident with new sanctions authorities the United States soon possessed (recounted below), pressure was easier to exert on Iran thereafter.

Economically, Iran was also in a powerful position up through 2010. As a major supplier of the world's oil during a time of high prices and perceived inventory shortages (in part stemming from ongoing conflicts in Iraq and Libya), Iran was in a position to play hardball over access to its oil resources. Moreover, Iran was and is a potentially major market, with 80 million people eager to engage with the international economy. As noted previously, the United States had been seeking to undermine this position for the entirety of the sanctions campaign. But that should not obscure the difficulty that was attached to the effort. Many states retained economic interest in Iran, and the nature of global competition made it especially difficult to convince a state that, were its companies and banks to abandon business in Iran, other states' firms would not "back-fill" and take advantage of newly opened market opportunities. This was particularly difficult to address in East Asia, where residual and historical tensions among China, South Korea, and Japan all reduced the ability of each state to trust the other. Shuttle diplomacy and clear messaging to all three parties was essential for the United States to persuade each to take steps that would contribute to U.S. sanctions efforts. Similar concerns also existed in Europe, though not always with respect to other

European countries' competition; oddly, many Europeans fixated on U.S. trade with Iran. Many European interlocutors voiced a concern that the United States only sought sanctions against Iran so as to open up its own opportunity for market share, implying that Iran would rather do business with U.S. firms in the event of a negotiated resolution to the crisis, especially if European companies were the last to exit Iran in difficult circumstances. My colleagues and I spent a good deal of time offering economic comparisons (noting, for instance, the vast difference in the types of goods sold to Iran from the United States—which were mostly agricultural—and the scale of business, which was mostly in the millions of dollars as compared to the billions involved in EU-Iran trade). Nonetheless, this argument persisted not only through the sanctions regime but also into JCPOA implementation and this notwithstanding the fact that the U.S. embargo remained almost completely intact even after the JCPOA.

In spite of these difficulties, the United States made some progress. From the end of 2010 through 2011, it steadily intensified pressure, with new sectors of Iran's economy coming under sanctions and a constant stream of new designations of Iranian bad actors. For example, in June 2011 (just a few weeks after I left the State Department for an assignment as Director for Iran at the National Security Council at the White House), the United States imposed sanctions on Tidewater Middle East Company, which was one of Iran's most important port operators, causing consternation in global trade as to whether or not any shipments to Iran could potentially be subject to U.S. penalties. They would not be, but the message was still a chilling one for international business. In November 2011, the United States imposed sanctions on the provision of support to Iran's petrochemical sector, which was one way Iran sought to evade U.S. pressure on other segments of the economy and was an increasingly important export market (to the tune of around ten billion dollars' worth of trade in 2011). Since petrochemicals used oil as a feed-stock element, targeting this sector also had the salutary effect of continuing to stigmatize oil and gas activities in Iran.

Still, the reality was that, though pressure was building on Iran, there were concerns both in the U.S. government and among some U.S. partners (particularly Israel) that the sanctions effort was not going fast enough to change Iran's nuclear calculus. In fact, during this period, Iran continued to install and operate new centrifuges, including more advanced machines, and was producing enriched uranium at various levels. The result of these developments was that Iran was steadily chipping away at the amount of "breakout" time the United States could count on in the event of an Iranian decision to acquire nuclear weapons. The result was an increasing clamor for either military action or intensified sanctions.

The Obama administration certainly preferred the diplomatic approach, augmented by tougher sanctions. This too was the U.S. Congressional focus. Here, however, there was a difference in view as to how best to structure new U.S. sanctions and their severity. The established narrative is that Congress, frustrated with a lackadaisical and hesitant Obama administration, pushed aggressive new sanctions on the executive branch, starting with those targeting Iranian oil exports in 2012. There is some truth to this, as Congress was a source of pressure on the administration to figure out how best to ramp up pressure on Iran. That said, the Obama administration was also trying to figure out how to target Iranian oil revenues at the same time, as well as how to target Iranian financial links more broadly. The problem was that we could not figure out a way of targeting oil or Iran's Central Bank that we deemed feasible and that would not potentially damage international oil markets and, thereby, set back the global recovery from the Great Recession of 2008–2009. It is hard to remember today, but the fragility of the international economy—and key U.S. allies—was significant. Moreover, some critical partners faced special circumstances, like Japan, which was recovering from the effects of the 2011 tsunami and resulting Fukushima nuclear disaster and nuclear power shutdown. Simply cutting off Iran's taps outright would have been foolish, counterproductive, and damaging to overall U.S. interests, including with regard to Iran. After all, if the United States were perceived as insufficiently careful, then the reaction from states around the world could well have been to ignore U.S. pressure, just as states did in the late 1990s. Moreover, if the result of increased U.S. sanctions pressure was an increase in oil prices, then we would have to work even harder to deprive Iran of the hard currency being generated by its oil sales. We had to identify a way to increase the pressure on Iran and only Iran, without spiking oil prices, damaging our economy and those of our partners, and accepting the blame for a crisis that could follow.

Congressional focus on this subject helped clarify administration debates on the matter, as Congress was intent on moving some kind of legislation forward. Negotiations between the legislative and executive branches resulted in the drafting of an ingenious compromise that neither side had in mind before November 2011: create a rationing system for Iran's oil purchasers, permitting them to continue buying Iranian oil (and have financial dealings with Iran's Central Bank) but with the amount purchased decreasing over time. This compromise, formalized in Section 1245 of the FY2012 National Defense Authorization Act, had three important components:

- It permitted the president to cut off the sanctions altogether if he determined that the global oil market could not sustain the loss of Iranian oil exports.
- It authorized exemptions from sanctions for those states that reduced their purchases of Iranian oil by "significant" amounts on a 180-day basis.
- It threatened a broad cut-off of financial institutions from the United States should the associated countries *not* make their 180-day reduction goals.

Even at a late date, the Obama administration urged Congress to leave this sanctions policy in the hands of the executive branch (failing miserably, to our chagrin). But there was no wavering in the administration's determination to press forward. Quickly, in January 2012, I led a process to assess whether sanctions could be implemented and what kind of reduction in Iranian oil revenue we would seek. The administration agreed at a senior level to push forward with the sanctions, although some in Congress erroneously and unfairly assumed the administration would simply use the presidential determination process to get out of sanctions, doubting that the administration had the stomach and interest to press forward despite ample evidence to the contrary. We also agreed to push for roughly 20 percent reductions from all oil exporters on a 180-day basis, even though we also sought higher reductions until an ill-timed letter and public advocacy campaign on the part of some members of the Senate and think-tank community undermined our negotiations with purchasers.[2] Next, we undertook a major campaign of diplomacy, information-gathering, and monitoring so as to oversee the implementation of these sanctions. We also sought to fix some of the errors and oversights in the underlying legislation with Executive Order 13622, authorized in July 2012 to—among other things—permit U.S. sanctions on the oil purchasers themselves, not just their associated banks.

The result was, by most measures, a tremendous success. Iran's economy went from GDP growth of 3 percent to a 6.6 percent contraction between 2011 and 2012 (figures 7.1 and 7.2).[3] Iranian unemployment and inflation remained in the double digits. In 2012, Iran's currency depreciated threefold in a matter of weeks, resulting in the hemorrhaging of Iranian hard-currency reserves.[4] Worse, these economic problems took place on top of unrealized economic expectations: it would have been one thing had Iran only dismal hopes for growth, but all this while, Iran enjoyed record oil prices and—in theory—should have been awash in oil revenues. International expectations for Iranian growth were also

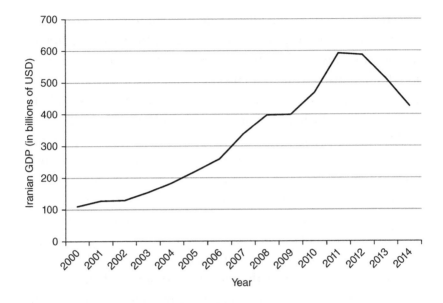

FIGURE 7.1 Iranian GDP, 2000–2014
Source: World Bank, World Development Indicators

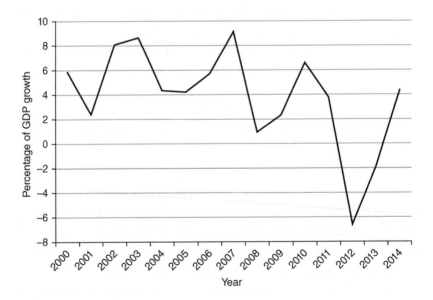

FIGURE 7.2 Iranian GDP growth rates, 2000–2014
Source: World Bank, World Development Indicators

dashed. Sanctions also impeded the economic reforms planned for the latter years of the Ahmadinejad presidency (2005–2013), which stalled in 2012 as a result of domestic political issues and the downward trajectory of the economy that removed flexibility and options for Iranian economic planners.

The United States took steps to ensure that these reforms would remain difficult to achieve, starting with the sanctions themselves as well as NOT imposing sanctions on things like humanitarian, consumer, or luxury goods that might have helped Iran reduce its import bills. With Iran's population technically able to purchase such goods and imports still flowing in, but with the exchange rate depriving most people of the practical benefit of being able to purchase these goods, only the wealthy or those in positions of power could take advantage of Iran's continued connectedness. Hard currency streamed out of the country while luxuries streamed in, and stories began to emerge from Iran of intensified income inequality and inflation (figure 7.3). This was a choice, a decision made on the basis of helping to drive up the pressure on the Iranian government from internal sources. The currency crisis in October 2012 helped crystalize this point, with Iranian protesters taking to the streets out of frustration over their meager take-home earnings. The United States and its partners used their knowledge of the Iranian revolution story and fear of economic discord as a deliberate way of prying apart the regime and the population, making the previously easy sell of the dignity of Iran's nuclear program far more costly.

Our sanctions campaign brought unforeseen, knock-on effects that played into our effort to increase the sense of pressure and unease within the Iranian economy. Some of these effects are little known, and they were not planned. But they may have been crucial in the shifting of Iranian government calculus and popular sentiment. Take, for example, rising chicken prices in 2012. The United States did not have sanctions in place against Iran's ability to import chickens. However, chicken prices tripled in 2012

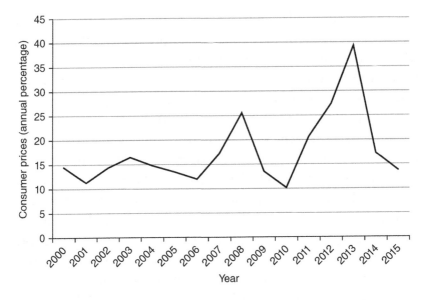

FIGURE 7.3 Iranian inflation rates, 2000–2015

Source: World Bank, World Development Indicators

due to inflation created by sanctions—built on Iranian economic mismanagement. This price hike may have contributed to more popular frustration in one bank shot than potentially years of financial restrictions.[5] This was particularly the case because the timing of sanctions interference with chicken supply happened to coincide with important Iranian holiday periods in which poultry is a major component (for American readers, imagine the price of turkey tripling in the middle of November). It undermined the sense of normalcy that Iran's leaders were intent on maintaining.

The United States took its surgical sanctions approach a step further in June 2013 with a carefully structured set of sanctions on Iran's automotive sector, denying Iran the ability to import manufacturing assistance but not spare parts for existing autos or whole cars themselves. Iranian manufacturing jobs and export revenue were the targets of this sanction, undermining the Iranian government's attempt to find non-oil export sectors and ways of employing 500,000 Iranians. All the while, the United States expanded the ability of U.S. and foreign companies to sell Iranians technology used for personal communications, helping ensure that the Iranian public had the ability to learn more about the dire straits of their country's economy and to communicate with one another, including a general license issued in late May.

Then, in early June 2013, the Iranian public elected Hassan Rouhani—who campaigned on a platform of economic reform and constructive foreign policy—as president.

Iranian Resolve

During this time and prior to Rouhani's election, Iran did not rest on its heels or accept its fate. Iranians responded by taking action that demonstrated resolve across each of the six resolve indicators described in chapter 6 (of course, they did not describe their response as such and many steps overlapped categories).

For example, the Iranians sought to maximize popular sentiment and regime support with respect to the nuclear issue. Propaganda measures were employed to maintain public support. For example, in 2007, the Iranian government began printing currency that explicitly acknowledged the nuclear program (with key facilities identified on a map of Iran on the back of the bill).[6] Then-president of Iran Mahmoud Ahmadinejad was particularly keen on this point creating new holidays in Iran to celebrate the country's nuclear achievements (Nuclear Day is April 9) and inaugurating some of the country's various nuclear facilities on multiple occasions. By making the nuclear program a subject of popular support, Ahmadinejad ensured that it would be impossible for either his government or a future one to accept a settlement of the nuclear issue that did not involve continuation of the program. This remains today a driver for the Iranian people. In 2007, 78 percent of Iranians favored development of nuclear energy.[7] In 2014, 75 percent of Iranians believed Iran should be able to develop its nuclear technology.[8] Nuclear technology was designated a birthright, its uranium resources became a sacred trust, and the achievements of its scientists were celebrated as those of the entire nation. Attacks on Iranian nuclear scientists by unclaimed assailants in 2011 and 2012 only reinforced these popular views, making the victims of apparent assassination into martyrs.

The Iranian government also sought to demonstrate economic normalcy for much of the sanctions period. They routinely touted favorable economic statistics while they remained such (as noted in chapter 6, including at meetings of the IMF) and similarly negotiated positive-sounding memoranda of understanding (MOUs) with countries around the world that gave the impression of an Iranian economy on the mend and on the move. The Iranians also used the opportunity afforded by international sanctions to debate a reform agenda that was intended to liberalize the economy and give it a bit more protection from outside forces.[9] At the same time, Iran also sought to strengthen its internal cohesion through appeals for an "economy of resistance" and to dilute the impact of sanctions through more direct evasion and smuggling initiatives. Iran also retaliated at times for the imposition of sanctions on its companies by infringing on the free operation of European and Asian companies, prohibiting certain European airlines from flying to Iran for a time after the EU prohibited a number of Iran Air flights into Europe over safety concerns.

Sanctions themselves also helped to push the Iranian economy in more positive directions. Take, for a moment, the U.S. attempt to reduce Iran's crude oil exports in 2012 and 2013. It imposed significant strain on the Iranian economy and probably contributed to the decision to seek a deal. As a contributor of 81.1 percent of GDP, the oil and gas exports sector held tremendous weight in 2011, and this helped to make it an attractive target.[10] But the imposition of sanctions pressure also contributed to the development of non-oil export products for Iran, namely cement.

This development helped insulate the government from some of the intermediate effects of oil-focused sanctions as did the more general drive to find new market opportunities in unsanctioned areas. Iran was able to build up a market presence in these commodities directly because sanctions reduced Iran's ability to export one good, prompting the development of another. Even beyond demonstrating resolve, such maneuvers added to Iran's ability to weather the sanctions storm.

On an international, political level, the Iranians continuously signaled their ability and readiness to resist demands to give up their nuclear program or to restrict it unduly. They did this in three central ways.

First, they corrected past mistakes in their cooperation with the IAEA and sought to portray the U.S. and partner campaign against Iran as a politically motivated witch hunt. This began early, starting in 2003 with Iran's decision to cooperate with the IAEA's investigation, accept implementation of enhanced monitoring and transparency rules (known in nuclear jargon as the "Additional Protocol"), and negotiate with the European Three (or EU-3, composed of France, Germany, and the United Kingdom). It even continued after Ahmadinejad became Iran's president, albeit in a more confrontational manner. As noted previously, Iran agreed to a Work Plan in 2007 under which it would provide some information to the IAEA and fill in a few gaps in the historical record, leaving some central issues—such as the extent of its past nuclear weapons program, something Iran has yet to acknowledge—for a later date. And Iran parceled out cooperation with the IAEA from that point forward, making access and transparency transactional rather than a prerequisite. (Ironically, it is this approach, which the Obama team inherited from the Bush administration and the IAEA Secretariat officials in charge at the time, that Obama's negotiators replicated in the JCPOA, meeting with significant criticism from some of the very same people involved in 2007.)

Second, acting within this international environment, the Iranians established clear lines about what they would and would not accept in a negotiated outcome. This in part derived from Iranian efforts to create an international environment in which they were perceived by many to be the victims rather than the aggressors. Iran co-opted genuine concerns among some nuclear "have nots" in the international community playing up the degree to which the Iran/ nuclear issue was actually a broader issue of nuclear rights rather than resolution of an issue prompted by Iranian misdeeds. They characterized their nuclear program as in keeping with the NPT and its provisions in Article IV for the sharing of nuclear technology with nonnuclear weapon states. This took place in a variety of fora, including the NPT Review Conferences in 2005 and 2010, as well as countless meetings of the Non-Aligned Movement and IAEA Board of Governors. These concerns existed before the Iran nuclear issue arose. But by wrapping its own cause in that of a more principled, thoughtful disagreement with how nuclear technology is shared around the world, Iran hoped to enlist the support of over a hundred states around the world for its cause and, to a certain extent, succeeded in doing so. The Iranians also played to their audience by announcing visits by IAEA inspectors and local Tehran diplomats to their nuclear sites, substituting genuine transparency and cooperation for stage-managed and unhelpful access. Moreover, they appealed to statistics to prove that they were more transparent than any other IAEA member, noting how many inspection hours they have endured in comparison to other states, while omitting the facts that those inspector hours were prompted by thirty years of nuclear noncompliance and were unsatisfactory in resolving said noncompliance.

Regardless, it worked, in that Iran was able to create an international sense of normalcy around its nuclear program that U.S. and partner negotiators had to accept as a given in both their sanctions drives and subsequent negotiating approaches with Iran. This sense of legitimization began with the first P5+1 offer to Iran

of May 2006, which indicated that "suspension" rather than termination of Iran's nuclear program would be sufficient UNSC
resolution 1737 reflected this agreement in its outlined conditions
for first the suspension of sanctions and then their termination,
none of which was predicated on the elimination of Iran's nuclear
fuel cycle. This legitimization was cemented with the second P5+1
offer of May 2008, which indicated that Iran's nuclear program
would be treated like any other state party of the NPT once confidence was restored.

Iran's effort in this respect was perversely aided by the U.S.
intelligence community. Though there were suspicions as late as
November 2007 that Iran's nuclear weapons program was active,
the U.S. intelligence community's assessment in the December
2007 National Intelligence Estimate (NIE) was that Iran had
halted its attempt to develop a nuclear warhead in 2003–2004
removed these suspicions and ended some of the sense of urgency
around Iran. There was evidence of a past attempt to develop a
nuclear warhead, which the International Atomic Energy Agency
concluded in December 2015 took place as part of "a coordinated
effort," and a careful read of the intelligence community's conclusion must acknowledge the United States believed Iran was
retaining a nuclear weapons "option."[11] But this nuance was often
dismissed with the blockbuster revelation that Iran's nuclear program was not as it was being sold by the United States.

Third, Iran continuously expanded its nuclear program, creating facts on the ground, but did not give the United States or its
partners the satisfaction of walking away from talks or from the
prospect of a negotiated outcome. There were certainly times
when I fervently hoped that Iran would make our job easier by
denying access to inspectors or even indicating its intent to withdraw from the NPT, for it would have been far more destructive
to U.S. efforts to isolate Iran had it simply accepted a suspension
of its nuclear program and then stalled on negotiations in per-
petuity. However, Iran did not oblige, conscious no doubt that

such a brazen act of defiance would empower the United States and our partners to bring immediate and withering pressure to bear on Iran.

Instead, Iran steadily built up its installed and operating centrifuges, enriched uranium at various levels, and constructed a reactor at Arak. That these steps were in defiance of UNSC resolutions was meaningful, legally, and served as a reminder for states around the world that Iran was acting at variance with its international obligations. Still, these legal issues did not swerve Iran in its construction of its capabilities. Doing so contributed to perceptions of its resolve and also helped it sustain a powerful message: that it would continue with its nuclear program, come what may.

Iran's actions had another benefit: creating new leverage and new cards to trade in a future negotiated solution. Just as the United States added to its collection of international sanctions, building up its own trade space for a future deal with Iran while creating pressure on Iran to seek that deal, Iran did the same: adding centrifuges to its combination of chits and creating pressure on the United States to seek a deal rather than face an Iran with a latent nuclear weapons capability.

At a Crossroads

By the summer of 2013, the United States and Iran (along with their partners around the world) were at an uneasy, uncomfortable, and unsustainable crossroads. For its part, Iran was successful at demonstrating a willingness to go to the wall in defense of its remaining nuclear program and to create enough uncertainty about the nature and extent of the problem that the Iranian preferred outcome—a deal in which they retained significant aspects of their existing nuclear program—was broadly accepted around the world. Iran had raised the stakes of its nuclear program, according it a higher status as a national interest than its intrinsic worth would suggest and—as a consequence—increasing the international perceptions that the country was not willing to forfeit a nuclear program with a full range of capabilities. The Iranians promulgated redlines with respect to any future nuclear agreement, starting with the proposition that further advances would have to be permitted unabated and that the nuclear program could take no single step back. Put another way, Iran was not only raising the stakes of the game with each new centrifuge but was also increasing the perceived value of each one.

On the other hand, the United States held the upper hand with respect to Iran's economy and the support of enough states around the world concerning the notion that Iran had an obligation to fulfill its nuclear commitments expeditiously. This support was limited and conditional, however, creating some limitations on the extent of international support for continued pressure on Iran. Even though states were concerned with Iran's nuclear program, most parts of the world did not believe the only way to address those concerns was for Iran to terminate its entire nuclear program.

Moreover, Iran's economy had already begun to stabilize in the summer of 2013, with inflation, unemployment, and currency depreciation leveling off after significant climbs. In addition, prospects for Iran's future isolation were limited by (1) the international oil market, which was already trading oil at record prices due to supply concerns; and (2) the already massive scope of existing sanctions provisions. If the Obama administration was going to make further progress in damaging the Iranian economy, then it would have to come from tools that would have undermined the health and welfare of the Iranian people (and possibly the global economy, given Iran's then supply of over a million barrels per day of oil in a tight oil market with high prices). Mindful of the experience of Iraq in the 1990s, very few people were supportive of instigating a humanitarian crisis in Iran or collapsing their own economies in the attempt.

For its part, Iran was by no means stable or secure. Having watched regional developments throughout the Arab Spring with a combination of glee and trepidation, the Iranian government was very conscious of the risk to its own stability that could come from further economic dislocation. Although Iran's economy had at least temporarily halted its death spiral after the election of Rouhani, it was by no means positioned to achieve much beyond marginal growth and potentially could fall back into dire straits. President-elect Rouhani soon had confirmed his worst fears that Iran's banking system was increasingly insolvent and that no combination of reforms could replace the essential need to dispose of economic sanctions. They were the fundamental roadblock for any future Iranian economic prosperity, on which he had based his election campaign and which more pragmatic Iranian officials staked their hopes for the sustenance of the Iranian system.

In 2013, therefore, both the United States and Iran saw tremendous uncertainty in the path forward and no guarantee their respective strategies would result in a satisfactory outcome for themselves. Instead, via secret talks that began in Oman and continued there, in Switzerland, and in New York, the United States and Iran sought to negotiate a way out of the dead end into which they were driving. I was privileged enough to be asked to join these talks, once more from a perch at the State Department, this time as the Deputy Sanctions Coordinator for the entire Department. My role was primarily to develop the sanctions-relief components of our negotiations with Iran, although—given my nuclear background—I also lent a hand in developing the types of restrictions and monitoring provisions that would be necessary for an agreement, as well as the sequence and pairing of any nuclear and sanctions components to a deal.

In the negotiations that followed, we and the Iranians focused on developing what was eventually described by others as a "win-win" outcome in which Iran would accept restrictions on its nuclear program and transparency provisions that went beyond its existing legal obligations under the NPT, in exchange for a relaxation of U.S. and other international sanctions. The first step of this process was concluded in November 2013 with the adoption of the Joint Plan of Action (JPOA) by the P5+1 and Iran. This was a carefully negotiated document, granting both sides some measure of respite from the pressures being applied by slowing down Iran's nuclear program in significant ways and easing sanctions pressure—but not too much. The JPOA was also deliberately incomplete in so far as a comprehensive settlement was concerned, leaving Iran needing more sanctions relief to repair its damaged economy and the United States and its partners in need of more permanent restrictions and transparency steps to have any confidence in the nature of Iran's nuclear program. The JPOA was then followed by laborious negotiations over the following twenty months, resulting in the Joint Comprehensive Plan of Action (JCPOA). In January 2016, the JCPOA was formally declared "implemented" by the P5+1 and Iran.

Both the JPOA and the JCPOA were subjected to rigorous scrutiny in the United States, in Iran, and in capitals throughout the international community. Both survived significant criticism. In Iran, the criticism focused on Iran's nuclear concessions, which were described by hardline elements of the population and government as a fundamental betrayal of Iran's national rights. In the United States, the criticism focused on how Iran's nuclear concessions were neither sufficiently deep nor long-lasting, and that sanctions relief would abet Iranian malicious activities in other ways (such as through the Iranian support of terrorism). Essentially, debate on this matter distilled down to two positions: (1) more pressure would eventually overwhelm Iranian nuclear commitment and resolve, and (2) more pressure probably wouldn't do so and there were profound risks in making the attempt, not least that Iran's nuclear program—and therefore the problem we were trying to solve—would grow.

A fundamental difference between the two positions was the degree of certainty expressed for them. Opponents of the JCPOA argued that more pain was achievable and would have the desired effect. Proponents did not discount that as a possibility but instead expressed concerns that if such a strategy did not work, then there would be less chance of making a diplomatic approach effective in the future because either additional sanctions pressure would be hard to come by or because Iran would not internalize it as desired. Ultimately, the fear in this camp was that the weight of sanctions was more likely to lessen in the future than tighten, resulting in a worse deal later than what was achievable in 2013 and 2015.

It is unknowable now whether opponents or proponents were right. Certainly, it is true that, after years of sanctions pressure, Iranian policy changed. One can debate the extent of the change, given allegations from the Iranian government that it was prepared to accept a more restricted nuclear program in 2005 than what emerged in the Joint Comprehensive Plan of Action, or the role played by sanctions. But, subsequent to the 2003–2005 diplomatic episode between Iran and the EU-3 in which such an offer was made, Iranian policy hardened into a knee-jerk defense of the nuclear fuel cycle and refusal to accept any abridgment, even on a temporary basis. This was not the same position taken in JPOA or JCPOA negotiations. Its perspective on its national priorities, as a consequence, must have shifted during the intervening time. Iran demonstrated over the period from 2006 to 2013 that its economic interests trailed the nuclear program in importance. By the time negotiations concluded on the JCPOA in 2015, Iran's sense of priorities—in the near term, if not permanently—had flipped, and it was prepared to accept limitations and monitoring on its nuclear program that were inconceivable in 2006. Given the role played by the Supreme Leader of Iran in making decisions on the talks and their outcome, it is not sufficient to conclude that a different Iranian president was responsible for the change. Moreover, some of the same people supportive of the JPOA and JCPOA in Tehran in 2013–2015 were opposed to even lesser confidence-building steps that President Ahmadinejad floated in the TRR proposal of 2009. Their positions changed in concrete terms.

That said, there were also limits on what Iran could accept as an outcome of the talks. The Iranians told U.S. negotiators consistently from the start of P5+1 talks in August 2013 that they would be prepared to consider temporary restrictions on the Iranian nuclear program, but not cessation and not restrictions that lasted for a considerable fraction of forever. This position was held constant, even as the precise limits of the Iranian negotiating position seemed to shift.

Many critics of the JCPOA have suggested that the U.S. team simply took the Iranian lines and accepted them as a given, without any form of pushback. This is not the case. The U.S. delegation spent months, often on its own, holding a tough line with respect to the acceptable extent of a future Iranian nuclear program (and even Iran's missile program). I am personally convinced that this position was essential in delivering the JCPOA as it was and that, had the United States not held firm, a deal would have been reached with Iran that fell short of the lines we established in the talks. Still, in time, it was clear from a variety of sources—including indicators outlined above—that while the Iranians had been pushed into modifying their positions and stepping off of their desired end state of sanctions termination without any further nuclear accommodation, they could not be swayed to accept just anything. The statements offered by Iranian negotiators corroborated this line of thinking, offering important clarification and reinforcement as to the nature of Iranian resolve but not conceding this core point. Though Iranian resolve had cracked, it had not fallen away.

With the Iran story told, it is worthwhile to examine why it occurred the way it did, as well as to seek a broader understanding of the inflection point that led to this outcome and how to structure a less ad hoc way of developing and executing sanctions.

8

On the Search for Inflection Points

IN THE PRECEDING CHAPTERS, we examined sanctions pain and resolve in isolation, identifying ways to classify and weigh the factors that go into these critical elements of leverage that both sides bring to a conflict. We also considered the case of Iran as it progressed. In this chapter, we will examine the effort to find intersection of these two forces, which ultimately is the trick of a sanctions campaign: subjecting a country to such pain that it concedes as swiftly as possible and modifies its behavior in a mutually acceptable (if not ideal) manner. I contend the JCPOA constitutes such an intersection of pain, resolve, and opportunity for a sanctioned country to get off the hook.

Reaching the "goldilocks" inflection point of effective sanctions pressure and resolve changes requires the development of a strategy for applying pain. Flowing from the issues discussed in prior chapters, I believe that it is necessary to design and implement sanctions following a framework introduced in the introduction and restated here. A state must

- identify objectives for the imposition of pain and define minimum necessary remedial steps that the target state must take for pain to be removed;

- understand as much as possible the nature of the target, including its vulnerabilities, interests, commitment to whatever it did to prompt sanctions, and readiness to absorb pain;
- develop a strategy to carefully, methodically, and efficiently increase pain on those areas that are vulnerabilities while avoiding those that are not;
- monitor the execution of the strategy and continuously recalibrate its initial assumptions of target state resolve, the efficacy of the pain applied in shattering that resolve and how best to improve the strategy;
- present the target state with a clear statement of the conditions necessary for the removal of pain and an offer to pursue any negotiations necessary to conclude an arrangement that removes the pain while satisfying the sanctioning state's requirements; and
- accept the possibility that, notwithstanding a carefully crafted strategy, the sanctioning state may fail because of inherent inefficiencies in the strategy, a misunderstanding of the target, or an exogenous boost in the target's resolve and capacity to resist. Either way, a state must be prepared either to acknowledge its failure and change its course or accept the risk that continuing with its present course could create worse outcomes in the long run.

In the simplest abstraction, we can imagine a scenario in which a sanction is applied, a target responds, and after one or two moves, the situation resolves itself as amicably as possible in these circumstances. One or both sides arrange for a climb-down by one or both sides, allowing for a settlement (permanent or not) and the removal of sanctions and establishment of a new normal. In fact, a survey of sanctions history—provided courtesy of Hufbauer, Schott, and Elliott—would argue in support of the notion that this is the prevailing pattern for sanctions implementation, with many modest sanctions regimes being imposed throughout the twentieth century and in short order being dismantled.

But the toughest cases rarely resolve themselves so neatly. This may be because sanctions are an altogether inappropriate tool to use in the situation at hand. However, basic neglect to adhere to a strategic framework in applying sanctions may also be involved, leading to the three most common causes of sanctions failure: under-reach, over-reach, and confused objectives.

Under-Reach

Sometimes, despite a sanctioner's best efforts, the imposition of sanctions does not generate the pain necessary to prompt a policy change. In fact, this is the base case for the imposition of sanctions pain until an inflection point is reached: sanctions imposition proceeds along its defined route, adding pain and inflicting damage along the way. And, at some stage, a switch is flipped and the state receiving the pain takes whatever step is necessary to prevent further pain.

However, there are some sanctions initiatives that never fulfill their objectives and modify the opposite state's behavior. An example of this could be the aforementioned Iranian decision to impose reciprocal sanctions on primarily European antagonists from 2006 to 2013. This step may have had political value at home, but from the standpoint of affecting the strategy of the sanctioned party—in these cases, to get them to withdraw the sanctions that they were applying against Iran—these sanctions were dismal failures.

Why they failed is an interesting question. The problem probably lies in the inadequacy of the sanctions imposed. The European economy was not sufficiently impinged in either case to prompt or justify policy reconsideration. Logically, this would argue in favor of Iran escalating their sanctions force in order to have the political impact desired. Yet, it did not do so. Instead, Iran continued to sell oil to and buy other things from Europe.

Two interlocking judgments are logical explanations for this outcome. The first is that Iranian officials assessed that their escalation of sanctions would diminish the readiness of Europe to stay the course and reject even tougher sanctions pushed upon them by the United States. From the policy statements made by European leaders on the Iranian file to the simple economic realities concerning the relative economic weight and opportunities available to Europe, it was apparent to many outside observers, and surely Iranian policymakers, that European resolve was unscathed and would remain so. But, for so long, neither was Europe prepared to abandon Iran altogether, choosing a middle course. An exaggerated Iranian sanctions campaign could have tipped this balance and away from Iran's own interest to retain some trade ties and relationships.

The second explanation is that the leaders of Iran understood that their country would be the worse for further escalation. From a compromised economic position, they determined that their own commitment in sustaining the application of pain against Europe would diminish over time, potentially undermining their ability to achieve a marginally better diplomatic solution. Consequently, rather than engage in a pointless and costly escalation, both took the more pragmatic and cautious route.

In abstract terms, the failure of a sanctions regime to achieve its initial objectives should logically prompt a reconsideration of those objectives by the sanctioning state. The question then becomes whether the sanctions endeavor is itself misguided or whether the tools are simply insufficient. As noted above, if a sanctioning party decides that the strategy may yet be successful if the sanctions regime is expanded, modified, or retargeted, then under-reach has yet to be "achieved"; rather, the reevaluation point simply becomes a bump in the road for the sanctions policy being implemented. On the other hand, a sanctioning party may decide that the strategy is fatally flawed and instead either modify it to employ new, tougher tools (such as military force) or change its objectives to align the existing tools with more plausible objectives. This reappraisal by the sanctioning state does not require a formal policy review, though it may involve one. Instead, it can merely begin with a leader's growing appreciation that the chosen path is not going to work.

Over-Reach and Unintended Consequences

Sanctions over-reach occurs when sanctions have been so onerous as to push the sanctions target to either double down on its existing, objectionable conduct or to escalate. Sanctions over-reach is a more complicated topic than sanctions under-reach, in part because it is less provable. Under-reach can be identified by the sanctions target's failure to change course. By contrast, over-reach can be easily argued by sanctions proponents and objective observers alike to be a manifestation not of an incorrect approach to sanctions but rather of the aggressive nature of the sanctions target. Just as with sanctions under-reach, the argument goes that sanctions "failed" because sanctions were an insufficient barrier to bad conduct—not that sanctions themselves prompted bad behavior.

But this mindset suggests that sanctions targets are not justified in seeing the imposition of sanctions as violence being inflicted against them by sanctioners. It substantiates a view—which I believe is wrongheaded—that sanctions are not strategically applied force but rather purely defensive measures applied by a sanctioning state to defend itself. As I have written about elsewhere, this argument is belied by both the rhetoric surrounding sanctions and the nature of the tools themselves and how they are implemented.[1]

If one instead thinks of sanctions as an instrument of force, then it is easy to understand how over-reach can occur and why the response to it can, at times, transcend economic or political means.

This is particularly the case when the application of sanctions is so damaging as to risk the primary motivations or interests of the target. A classic example of this is the imposition of the U.S. oil embargo against Japan in the 1930s. Some commentators have argued that this action led the Imperial Japanese government to fear for its economic survival and, in time, to attack Pearl Harbor in 1941.[2] For the United States, however, the embargo was a signal of resolve and warning to Japan, while it simultaneously choked off a supply of vital materiel for the Japanese war effort. What the United States failed to understand is that Japan saw this action as itself a casus belli. A similar argument can be made to the over-reach of economic force against Germany during the interwar period, albeit in the form of "reparations."

Of course, the problem with the possibility of sanctions over-reach is that it argues for restraint on the part of sanctioners if there is a chance that the sanctioned party will overreact. Yet, the power of sanctions depends—at least in part—on the perceived threat of escalation on the part of the sanctions target. If targets believe things can get better or if they can accommodate themselves to the pain, then sanctions lose their potency. To some extent, the challenge faced by sanctioners is the same as those facing their military counterparts in the conduct of a limited war. Without the specter of complete annihilation to compel capitulation, sanctions targets may be less willing to compromise in the short term, prolonging the crisis and the conflict. With that specter, then it is possible the sanctions target will instead mount a counteroffensive that exceeds the risk tolerance of the sanctioner or—worse—respond in other ways, just as the Japanese did in 1941.

There is no hard-and-fast trick for divining when sanctions may transcend their intended level of distress and become instead a trigger for the target state to lash out. Rather, success lies in a careful examination of the interests of the target and in knowing how far to push. The approach suggested with respect to measuring resolve is also helpful here, as the sorts of analysis required to understand whether a target is about to fold can also point to indications that a target is about to instead escalate the situation. But, ultimately, it is this possibility that ought to make sanctions proponents pause in their advocacy.

Another risk from sanctions over-reach is the creation of unintended (and, ultimately, unproductive) pain for the sanctions target. Any foreign policy action carries with it some risk of unintended consequences. These consequences can have a strategic flavor: for example, that the decision to undertake one military mission deprives a force of the ability to undertake another, even if the second mission is more vital to the future of the state in question. Sanctions too can share this risk: using sanctions to reduce the ability of one major oil exporter to put oil on the market means that the market itself is less able to weather the withdrawal of another oil producer's share.

But in sanctions, the unintended consequence most frequently cited is that of humanitarian suffering. As described in chapter 2, "Iraq in the 1990s" has become the poster child for the concept of sanctions imposing undue humanitarian consequences, with hundreds of thousands of Iraqis bearing the brunt of the economic deprivation imposed as a result of sanctions and Iraqi government policy in response to them. Even sanctions regimes with humanitarian carve-outs can contribute to humanitarian problems because of the broader effects of the measures selected. In Iran, for instance, there were reports throughout 2012 and 2013 that medicine and medical devices were unavailable not because their trade was prohibited but rather because they cost too much for the average Iranian due to shortages and the depreciation of the Iranian currency.[3] The United States and its partners, through sanctions, directly contributed to the depreciation of the Iranian rial and, consequently, played some part—even if unintentional— in the creation of this problem.

Sanctions over-reach of this sort is not merely an issue for aid workers. Misdirected sanctions pressure can also undermine the utility of a sanctions regime by stiffening resolve (aiding the government targeted to pin the blame on an outside other rather than accept the blame for its own misdeeds) and create a vicious cycle of deepening resentment toward the outside world. Sanctioners should be wary of—and responsive to, where possible—indications that their sanctions regime is having significant unintended consequences because these effects could be counterproductive in both the short and long term.

The U.S. effort to target Iran via the Islamic Revolutionary Guard Corps (IRGC) is an instructive case in point. From 2006 to 2010, much of the U.S. strategy was to identify the litany of misdeeds undertaken by the IRGC and to extrapolate from there a basis to isolate Iran economically. The approach was straightforward (and aided by Iranian conduct): show that the IRGC was a bad actor and urge partners to forbid any economic activities with it or its proxies. In time, this strategy took on additional elements. Legally, the United States decided that any significant transactions with the IRGC and its associates merited being cut off from the U.S. financial system (via the 2010 Comprehensive Iran Sanctions, Accountability and Divestment Act [CISADA]). Diplomatically, the United States broadened the sweep of its condemnation of the IRGC, adding it to a variety of different sanctions lists, with elements designated under U.S. law for violations of human rights, actions in Syria, testing of ballistic missiles, and so forth. The IRGC, already powerful in Iran domestically, was also portrayed by Washington as being at the center of all Iranian government conduct. Again, this claim had a factual basis. But the intent of the U.S. strategy was to make the IRGC and Iran inseparable concepts with the aim of chilling even still legal forms of business with Iran under the precept that no one could know outside Iran whether the IRGC was involved in or the beneficiary of transactions at a deep level.

Although U.S. sanctions targeted the IRGC explicitly, the IRGC arguably grew stronger during this period. Why? I believe two factors explain this situation. The first is that IRGC officers were in a good position to capitalize on the inherent corruption of the Iranian economy that was enriched by a negligent Ahmadinejad administration of 2005 through 2013. They possessed the connections and the wealth to place themselves at the center of the Iranian economy, using available funds to take significant if not controlling stakes in a variety of Iranian economic concerns. Second, ironically, U.S. sanctions and hostility toward the IRGC forced the Iranian system both to rely upon and to support the IRGC. The IRGC was a primary means whereby Iran could procure sensitive items otherwise prohibited under sanctions, making the IRGC once more heroes to the Iranian government and the economic beneficiaries of their smuggling enterprise. For this reason, as Iran grew poorer and more vulnerable to economic pressure, the IRGC grew stronger.

This reality has made JCPOA implementation especially difficult because international business cannot escape the possibility that sitting at the other end of even legitimate transactions was a very illegitimate actor. Even under the JCPOA, the IRGC is not due to be removed from U.S. sanctions, exposing non-Iranian business to the risk of being punished for violations of U.S. sanctions. For this reason, the U.S. Department of the Treasury took the somewhat extraordinary step of indicating that even transactions with IRGC-controlled entities might not necessarily be sanctionable during an update to standing legal guidance in late 2016. However, as a Reuters analysis showed in January 2017, the beneficiaries of many foreign deals with Iran under the JCPOA still involved the IRGC at some level.[4]

Predictably, this has led to charges that while advocates of the JCPOA hoped it would lead to economic openness in Iran that is counter to IRGC and state-level control, the opposite has proven true, at least in the short term. Given the hostility and fear that—again, justifiably—still surrounds the IRGC in the United States and broader international community, it can be safely concluded that the U.S. sanctions focus on the IRGC in the early period of enforcement did little to damage the IRGC. Instead, it may have contributed to lagging implementation of the JCPOA. Worse, since the IRGC's response to sanctions was to place itself more at the center of Iranian affairs, the U.S. approach toward the IRGC ultimately could have helped reinforce the IRGC's grip over the country.

Importantly, this was not a surprise to many analysts looking at Iran from 2006 to 2016, including some in the U.S. government. Ultimately, the exigencies of the situation forced this kind of strategy on the United States and its partners. Indeed, while it is possible that an IRGC sanctions focus may have limited the sanctions relief of the JCPOA to Iran, it is also possible that a different sanctions approach may have failed to generate the pressure necessary to achieve the JCPOA. My aim with this observation is not to suggest that the United States should have chosen a different approach to the sanctions regime in 2006–2010 but rather to underscore the point that second- and third-tier implications from sanctions actions are sometimes difficult to predict. Given this, the unintended consequences of sanctions merit considerable study both in academia and by sanctions practitioners. They should observe the IRGC situation and keep it in mind as they develop future sanctions regimes.

Confused Objectives

In the previous sections, I make a prevailing assumption: that the sanctioner pursues a uniform, commonly understood set of objectives. In many cases, this is probably true. The sanctioner may not be able to achieve its goal, but it knows what it is trying to do and—consequently—has a clear set of thresholds that sanctions help it cross.

But this is probably not universally true, and the cases of Iraq and Iran neatly demonstrate this particular problem. For Iraq, the goals identified at the start of the sanctions campaign were straightforward: end Iraq's ability to threaten its neighbors with weapons of mass destruction and prevent further aggression from Saddam Hussein. Over time, the objective shifted: it was no longer acceptable to contain Saddam Hussein—in part because of fears that the sanctions regime might fade away—because he was deemed uncontainable. Instead, the only acceptable objective that could be attained was Saddam's removal from power. By realizing this objective, Iraq would be able to once more become a trustworthy nation. As a result, the ultimate goal of defanging Iraq would be achieved.

The problem is that sanctions pressure—even combined with the threat of force—was insufficient to motivate Saddam to depart Iraq before hostilities were begun in March 2003. The shifting objectives of sanctions—from containing the menace that Iraq could become to ensuring that it would never be in a position to menace its neighbors—simply increased the burden that sanctions pressure and the threat of force were forced to bear. And, by setting the bar so high, U.S. and partner decision makers almost ensured that nonmilitary means to achieve the goal would be a failure, particularly when it became apparent that the pressure the United States and partners sought to apply on Saddam Hussein simply was being shrugged off through sanctions evasion and Saddam's deliberate lack of concern for the plight of his population.

With Iran, a similar murkiness clouded deliberations over the goals and related objectives of the nuclear-related sanctions campaign. In its most direct formulation, the U.S. goal was for Iran to be prevented from producing or acquiring a nuclear weapon. That Iran would have a latent nuclear weapons capability was ensured by its successful operation of a uranium centrifuge facility during the last years of the George W. Bush administration. Iran would be capable, even if its existing facilities were destroyed, of resurrecting its nuclear weapons program at a time and place of its choosing. I would argue that the George W. Bush administration was not solely responsible for Iran's standing at the nuclear precipice and that, as outlined in chapter 3, Iran achieved a significant degree of latency with its clandestine acquisition of uranium centrifuges in the late 1980s and illicit experiments with them in the 1990s. The task for the George H. W. Bush, Clinton, George W. Bush, and Obama administrations was to seek a solution for Iran's nuclear program that kept it from physically developing nuclear arms and from politically deciding to pursue them.

By 2009, a healthy debate had emerged in Washington, as well as in capitals throughout the Middle East, as to whether this established goal could be achieved through nonmilitary means. There were advocates for and against, with perspectives ranging from a conviction that, even if sanctions compelled Iran to make concessions, Iran could never be trusted with any form of nuclear program because the risk of its cheating was too strong. This debate also involved a more fundamental question about the nature of the Iranian government. Some passionately believed (and many still believe) that the present system of Iranian government is incompatible with good relations with the West or its regional neighbors. To varying degrees, they believe that regime change in Iran is a necessary precondition of a sustainable Middle Eastern security and political order, and that a change in the Iranian government would be better for the Iranian population, as well. For the analysts and politicians of this school of thought, sanctions were a vital component of a broad strategy for confronting Iran's full range of bad behavior. Until and unless each constituent element of that bad behavior was resolved, a negotiated solution involving sanctions relief for Tehran was inherently suspect. Some in this camp may have been prepared to accept modest modifications to U.S. sanctions policy, mindful of Iranian politics. Others may have been prepared to acknowledge that some fundamental elements of Iranian policy would remain unchanged in any deal negotiated. For example, they might have acknowledged that the internal Iranian human rights situation may not improve as a result of a nuclear deal but that—in addition to addressing issues around the Iranian nuclear program—Iran must make an accommodation with respect to its support for Hezbollah in order to receive sanctions relief.

By contrast, others—including the Obama administration, in general—accepted a different logic. It started with certain assumptions about the problem facing the United States and its partners, and the likelihood of sanctions—or, for that matter, external pressure as a general matter—changing Iranian policies and practices across the board. For these analysts and politicians, it was necessary to have a more constrained vision for what sanctions could do and what U.S. policy could achieve. Few, if any, of these individuals would offer any acceptance of Iran's range of destructive and loathsome activities. Most, in fact, would freely stress their opposition to Iran's behavior in this regard. But they had a different understanding of what the sanctions regime assembled from 1996–2013 was intended to achieve and what was possible even under ideal circumstances. Consequently, they had another vision for the JCPOA and a different way of gauging its success. Moreover, some (me included) argued that a different strategy, with economic and political engagement at its core rather than isolation, would be more effective in addressing Iran's internal political and human rights situation and that different tools (like maritime interdictions) would be more successful in controlling Iran's support for terrorism abroad.

For a while, the combination of threatened U.S. military force and a largely unified, global approach to sanctions papered over this debate, as everyone in Washington (and beyond) opposed to Iranian nuclear weapons development could find something in the U.S. and partner strategy to latch onto. This papering over was facilitated by a holistic approach to sanctions, with measures imposed against Iranian individuals and entities for a variety of bad acts. In some cases, as with the IRGC, certain entities were targeted multiple times via multiple legal instruments, even if they had overlapping penalties. By throwing the book at the IRGC and others in Iran, the strongest case possible was made that Iran's many bad acts merited international isolation. However, although it made sense at the time, this was a tactical mistake on the part of the Obama administration and one that helped create the problems that emerged with the negotiations effort from 2013 to 2016.

In my view, this debate re-erupted with the JCPOA because the objectives of the sanctions strategy were confused and obscured. Each side in the debate, both for the deal and against it, could argue that the other side was misunderstanding the purpose of the sanctions effort and come to a different conclusion as to whether sanctions relief in the JCPOA was appropriate. This became doubly complicated when it became apparent that, in addition to confused objectives, there was a difference in analysis as to how far sanctions could push Iran to make concessions. For some, the sky was the limit. Others accepted the limited—though real—utility of sanctions power against Iran.

Ultimately, the debate crystallized around supposition from all sides, argued in a polarized political environment. No one can be proven right, in part because all sides are arguing counterfactual points on the basis of their analysis of an uncertain future.

But these competing views of reality must be reconciled if there is to be an acceptable basis of fact on which to evaluate such an important policy decision as the JCPOA despite the myriad objectives pursued. The question is not whether the JCPOA itself is good; rather, the question is whether additional pressure could have gotten something "better," defined here as an increase in the scope, duration, or severity of the restrictions in place against Iran under the JCPOA or modifications to its broader range of illicit activities.

Proponents of the JCPOA assert that that more sanctions pressure would not have resulted in a better deal if it were even possible to create such pressure. As I noted in earlier chapters, many proponents argue that, at the time JCPOA negotiations were commenced, sanctions pressure against Iran was beginning to wane and expectations in the country had improved. Much of the reasoning for this judgment is tied to the election of President Hassan Rouhani in June 2013 and his appointment of a range of technocratic experts to govern the country. But part of the reasoning stems from the plateau that sanctions pressure had apparently reached by fall 2013. A variety of indicators support this contention, which even opponents of the JCPOA have acknowledged to some extent (at a minimum, in their insistence in fall 2013 that sanctions be intensified). Three indicators worth outlining here are: the increased stability of Iranian oil exports, albeit at a significantly lower level than in 2011 and previous (captured in figure 8.1); increase in non-oil trade with Iran (captured in table 8.1), albeit not at a sufficient rate to make up for lost oil revenues; and the efficiencies achieved as a result of reforms undertaken prior to 2013—such as reduced subsidies for and price controls over energy products— and what was planned insofar as future privatization.

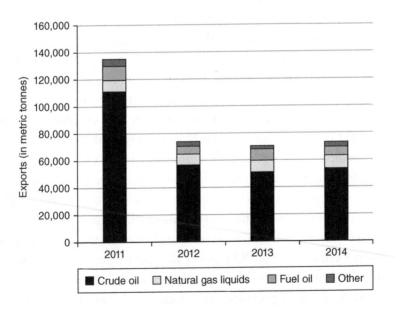

FIGURE 8.1 Iran's trade balance, 2011–2014 (in $U.S. millions)

Source: IMF 2014 Article IV Consultation on Iran, 2014

Table 8.1 Iran's Trade Balance, 2011–2016 (in $U.S. millions)

	2011–12	2012–13	2013–14 (Est.)	2014–15 (IMF staff)	2015–16 (IMF staff)
Trade balance	67,068	30,975	32,761	26,192	18,000
Exports	144,873	98,033	93,560	92,226	88,524
Oil and gas	118,231	62,916	56,328	52,754	46,472
Crude oil	93,725	44,345	37,837	34,555	29,482
Petroleum products and natural gas	24,506	18,571	18,491	18,199	16,990
Non-oil and gas	26,642	35,117	37,231	39,472	42,052
Imports	−77,805	−67,058	−60,799	−66,034	−70,524

Source: IMF Article IV Consultation on Iran, 2014

The pain expectation for proponents of the JCPOA, therefore, did not stay in a plateau: it started to drop. The expectation among policy makers is that it would do so absent the kind of embargo placed on Iraq in the 1990s and possibly with the same sorts of consequences. Policy makers were also concerned with the risk of sanctions fatigue sapping support behind the policy and Iran receiving the benefit of sanctions relief for free. Plain economics were a part of this calculation in addition to strategy: at the time negotiations started with Iran in 2013, oil was still trading at more than $100 per barrel.

But proponents of the JCPOA did not merely argue that the application of pain could not be intensified; they also contended that opponents of the JCPOA misunderstood the intensity of Iranian resolve. This argument focused on three themes: first, Iran was prepared to accept considerable hardship in defense of its nuclear program, which had become a national treasure; second, Iran believed that it could outwait the United States and its partners, reducing its incentive to negotiate and increasing its incentive to build facts on the ground with new centrifuge installations; and, third, the degree to which Iran is incapable of compromising with its hated American enemy, particularly on issues associated with its regional and domestic policies. These three factors combined to create a resolve perspective in Iran that was intrinsically opposed to capitulation in negotiations and, thereby, a limit to how far Iranian negotiators would be prepared to go.

Proponents of the JCPOA argued that it was possible that additional pressure could create a better JCPOA, but that it was unknown if and how much more pressure would be required to overwhelm Iranian resolve. And, to boot, opponents were unable to articulate what kind of negotiated outcome Iran could reasonably be expected to support that would meet the standards demanded by those in opposition. Still, opponents of the JCPOA, by contrast, expressed confidence that the inevitability of economic decline in Iran would force further concessions on the part of Iranian negotiators, if not immediately, then in time, given Iranian worries about domestic unrest from continued sanctions pressure. Ironically, both proponents and opponents of the JCPOA drew confidence in their positions from a common conclusion that pressure had an impact; the questions became how much more impact could be achieved and to what end.

Opponents, however, did not acknowledge the degree to which this approach failed in Iraq. It was on this basis that the Obama administration argued military conflict probably would result from failing to accept the JCPOA when negotiations concluded: Iran's resolve to prevent full restrictions on its nuclear program would generate an inevitability for war, as was the case in Iraq. Iranian refusal to cooperate would signal bad intent for the long term, which further restrictions might not address. Only regime change and military action could achieve the desired results of full assurance. This point is particularly crucial, as it formed another crux of the debate: the established risk tolerance of future Iranian nuclear pursuits of opponents to the JCPOA was so low as to create an impossible standard for negotiations, just as it was with Iraq in 2003. The logic of their own positions would force, in all but the most inconceivable scenarios of Iranian capitulation, a conclusion that Iran had not conceded enough in order to be trusted. And, for this reason, their opposition was seen to be less on the merits of the JCPOA or the sanctions regime that helped create it, and more on the entire concept of a negotiated outcome.

Measuring levels of pain and resolve therefore took on significance that was not hitherto experienced in sanctions-related debates. Prior to the Iran deal, many sanctions cases resulted in the petering out of sanctions pressure prior to either collapse of the sanctions regime or onset of military force. Otherwise, it resulted in a dramatic escalation into military force after a short time. Here, in the Iran case, was a rare event: the negotiated conclusion of a cease-fire in which weapons were not fired. But in a normal cease-fire, there is clarity as to the nature of the stakes facing antagonists; with the Iran deal, the picture was (and is) cloudier.

Goldilocks

The strategy of sanctions rests on a fundamental pillar: that a combination of pressures can be applied on a state to overcome its resistance and get it to change its policy.

It is difficult to identify the point at which sanctions pressure and target resolve are sufficiently balanced to create the compromises and concessions sought. The difficulty lies in part because the risk of sanctions under-reach and over-reach remain tied to the perspective of the sanctioning jurisdiction. But it is also because there will always remain imperfection in the information available to both sanctioner and target, as well as in their analysis in how the situation will progress absent a resolution. Assuming there is a moment (or, more likely, moments) in which resolve and pain are balanced and it is advantageous to cut a deal for both sides, the task is to analyze how resolve and pain interact.

The existence of such a perfect "inflection point" revolutionizes analysis of the relationship between sanctioner and sanctioned, making their competition a battle of time, resources, and will. For the sanctioner, the game becomes increasing pain to reduce resolve as swiftly as possible. For the sanctioned party, the endeavor naturally becomes keeping its resolve from draining away. Both have several options available to them to pursue such a strategy—from enlisting partners to targeting vulnerabilities in the target economy or sanctioner's legal regime—but the precise tools are less important for us to consider at this stage. It is merely sufficient to accept that they exist and will be employed.

It is here that the framework we've been building is so important, as it gives the sanctioner the clearest picture possible of the interests, desires, vulnerabilities, and weaknesses of its targets. It permits a sanctioner to assemble a profile of its target, highlighting those points and identifying means to do damage to the target. It suggests how much time should be allotted for sanctions to do their work and to what degree the use of time itself as a weapon may be effective (such as in the oil-reduction effort against Iran) and to what degree allowing time to pass could eventually undermine the sanctions regime (as the oil reduction effort against Iran may have become absent the negotiation and implementation of the JPOA). Done properly, it also identifies areas to hit and to avoid, either because applying pain would be counterproductive or meaningless for the final result, just as someone skilled in martial arts can identify pressure points and render their opponent defenseless.

This latter point is a crucial element in particular of the targeted sanctions movement, which probably has not gotten enough credit from those concerned about the humanitarian implications of sanctions. True, even targeted sanctions can eventually cause humanitarian problems. For example, the aforementioned rise in chicken prices in Iran was not exclusive to poultry but affected all manner of agricultural and medical goods, in addition to run-of-the-mill consumer products. Inflation can be modulated with price controls, but, absent that, it tends to strike a variety of goods equally. Sanctions that aim to increase inflation de facto aim to increase costs to average citizens. But with targeted sanctions, the goal of shifting an adversary's policy is modulated with a desire to do so in the most efficient and effective manner possible. This did not occur with Iraq in the 1990s but largely did take place in the case of Iran. Whether the analytical framework developed and considered here can be applied to this end in other cases is the subject of the next chapter.

9

Looking Ahead

AT THE CLOSE OF the Obama administration, sanctions remained a preeminent tool for U.S. national security and foreign policy. They were mentioned as a core instrument of national power multiple times in the 2015 National Security Strategy, with the longest mention meriting reproduction in full here [emphasis added]:

> At the same time, we will exact an appropriate cost on transgressors. Targeted economic sanctions remain an effective tool for imposing costs on those irresponsible actors whose military aggression, illicit proliferation, or unprovoked violence threaten both international rules and norms and the peace they were designed to preserve. We will pursue multilateral sanctions, including through the U.N., whenever possible, but will act alone, if necessary. *Our sanctions will continue to be carefully designed and tailored to achieve clear aims while minimizing any unintended consequences for other economic actors, the global economy, and civilian populations.*

In many cases, our use of targeted sanctions and other coercive measures are meant not only to uphold international norms, but to deter severe threats to stability and order at the regional level.[1]

As of the time of this writing, the future direction of U.S. sanctions strategy is unclear. Donald Trump's election in 2016 has called into question the degree to which the United States will be prepared to weaponize its economy in the future. As a business-person whose cabinet is staffed with other business people, Trump could be expected to oppose those foreign policy responses that leverage and put at risk access to the U.S. economy, as well as the opportunities of U.S. business abroad. On the other hand, Trump's campaign was replete with threats to do precisely that, although with the objective of strengthening the U.S. domestic manufacturing and industrial sectors rather than achieving specific foreign policy objectives. And Trump is not the only U.S. government decision-maker; Congressional enthusiasm for sanctions is unabated, even when Trump disagrees, as was the case with the passage of the Countering America's Adversaries Through Sanctions Act in July 2017.

Rather than project Trump's future decisions—which is impossible at the time of this writing given the inconsistency of his positions—in this chapter, we will examine three cases for which sanctions have thus far been assigned a role at the end of 2016 and which were the subject of the July legislation: Iran's regional bad behavior and violations of Iranian human rights, Russia's infringement of Ukrainian sovereignty, and North Korea's nuclear weapons program. I offer ways of thinking about these three problems and the utility of sanctions in dealing with them. I use the framework presented in the introduction and developed throughout this book to recommend how the United States and its partners *ought* to respond rather than how they necessarily *will* respond.

Iran

Having spent much of this book describing my experience with U.S. sanctions policy toward Iran, I will not reinvest substantial time or pages in offering additional background here. Rather, it is sufficient to say that Iran's activities throughout the Middle East and at home continue to be of concern for the United States, its partners and allies in the region, and beyond. These activities include providing physical and financial support to groups that the United States considers terrorist organizations (such as Hezbollah) and others that are imperiling the stability of countries around the region (such as Syrian president Bashar al-Assad and the Yemeni Houthis). It is these activities that, as mentioned in chapters 7 and 8, led to disagreement within the U.S. political and analytic establishment about whether to support or oppose the Joint Comprehensive Plan of Action (JCPOA) and which have raised questions about the continuation of the JCPOA into the Trump administration.

The JCPOA continues to have real value for the United States in that it constrains Iran's ability to develop nuclear weapons and to make advances toward them that could undermine regional national security perceptions. As the United States frequently noted during the sanctions campaign that preceded the JCPOA, if governments around the Persian Gulf and beyond are concerned about Iran without nuclear weapons, how much greater and deeper would be their fears about an Iran either in possession of or poised to acquire such arms. From this perspective, regional states too have an interest in the JCPOA being maintained, as Prince Turki al-Faisal, a prominent Saudi national security thinker, noted in November 2016.[2]

If we assume that maintaining the JCPOA remains a priority for the United States as well as our partners, then a strategy to confront Iran (including through the use of sanctions) over its other bad acts needs to be developed. And it should exclude measures that contravene the terms of the JCPOA. The framework presented throughout this book can serve this purpose.

First, we must identify objectives for the imposition of pain and define minimum necessary remedial steps that Iran must take for pain to be removed. In this case, we can identify three:

- Elimination or significant reduction of military and financial support to regional groups threatening the stability or integrity of existing states, and a commitment not to engage in such support in the future. This can and should include countries like Yemen, Bahrain, Iraq, and Saudi Arabia (where, even if Iranian involvement is minimal, it is suspected by Saudi authorities to be significant), as well as Palestinian terrorist groups. Ideally, it would also include groups like President Assad of Syria and Hezbollah, though international support for such an identification is less likely to be successful.
- Cooperation with the United Nations Special Rapporteur for Human Rights in Iran and meaningful steps to address concerns regarding the human rights of the Iranian population, including religious minorities and other at-risk populations.
- Cooperation with international efforts to address global terrorist threats, such as al Qaeda and ISIS. This could include surrendering al Qaeda members who may be located in Iranian territory for prosecution in their home jurisdictions, as well as participating in global efforts to eradicate such threats.

Second, we must understand as much as possible Iran's vulnerabilities, interests, commitment to support acts of terrorism and violations of human rights within its territory, and readiness to absorb pain in support of these policies.

Clearly, after more than ten years of an active sanctions posture, the United States and international community know Iran's vulnerabilities to sanctions well. Oil and gas remain its two most important industries, with a few climbing up the ladder—petrochemicals, automotives, and perhaps consumer goods—but yet to rival hydrocarbons. The reform agenda in Iran is proceeding, albeit on shaky ground given the nature of the privatization debate (with some major power brokers, like the IRGC, concerned about their role in a new Iranian economy). And Iran's financial sector remains incredibly fragile, and on the cusp of insolvency due to a legacy of bad debts and weak investment. Relief from sanctions under the JCPOA has yet to permit Iran's leadership to restore real confidence in the sector. From this perspective, Iran remains vulnerable to sanctions pressure though our options to use this vulnerability against Iran in this way are constrained by the JCPOA.

But we also know that Iran has demonstrated significant resilience in the face of efforts to address the problems it creates regionally, even if the full reach of sanctions was possible. Iran was named a State Sponsor of Terrorism in the United States in 1984. The comprehensive U.S. embargo followed in 1995 in response to Iranian support for terrorist attacks around the world, which the 1996 attack on Khobar Towers in Saudi Arabia (killing 19 U.S. airmen and injuring over 350 other people) reinforced as a persistent aspect of Iranian regional policy. As I have written elsewhere, Iran continued to support terrorism and engage in policies that violate Iranian citizens' human rights despite some of the most intense economic sanctions ever devised, some of which were imposed directly in response to these activities.[3] This is in part because these activities either have direct value to Iran for the maintenance of the regime (as in the case of egregious human rights behavior) or tremendous importance as part of Iran's foreign policy (as with support for activities the United States considers terrorism). In addition, these activities are relatively low cost. Sanctions can choke off a billion-dollar nuclear program requiring a global supply chain much more easily than

148

a million-dollar aid program involving point-to-point transfers to a terrorist proxy.

Moreover, given the dynamics of Iran's internal politics, backing away from such support for violent extremism or desisting in human rights violations could be conceived of as creating vulnerability where none exists. It is certainly possible that the Iranian population would continue to support an entity known as the Islamic Republic of Iran even without the *Basij* militia and security forces. But it is doubtful that the regime would dominate its population without such apparatus. Consequently, from a national policy perspective, Iran's leaders could see great vulnerability being *created* from cooperating with U.S. and other foreign attempts to improve human rights in Iran. Likewise, even though they too may support groups like Hezbollah, reformers probably see risk in removing from the hands of security-minded Iranian politicians the tool of foreign influence-building through supporting such groups. Given this, Iran would have to weigh— and those imposing sanctions against Iran would similarly have to consider—the relative extent of existing vulnerabilities that might be created by any particular outcome of a negotiation.

Third, we should develop a strategy to carefully, methodically, and efficiently increase pain on those areas that are vulnerabilities, while avoiding those that are not.

Unlike the nuclear issue, which was of limited national consciousness until Iran's leaders elevated its place in political discourse in the 2000s, developing a sanctions strategy that threatens Iranian national interest to obtain concessions on terrorism or human rights could be much more difficult to achieve.

To be effective, the sanctions strategy will have to internalize the likelihood (if not the certainty) that merely applying pressure on Iran's leadership and economy and expecting the Iranian government to back away from its support for Hezbollah will not work. Iran has absorbed considerable pressure in the past and persisted in its pernicious activities. It is certainly true that the United States has yet to organize a comprehensive, global embargo against Iran. It is similarly true that Iran's response to such an embargo would be to concede such activities. However, even if we take on board the dubious prospect of sanctions pushing Iran to abandon Hezbollah altogether, securing such an embargo would require a degree of global consensus around the nature of Iran's bad acts that has thus far eluded both Republican and Democratic presidents. It is notable, for example, that although the United States has had sanctions against Hezbollah for decades, only in the past five years did the European Union impose sanctions on the organization and, even then, only against the "military wing" of Hezbollah. Bearing in mind the relative ease through which resources can be passed from one "wing" to another, such a specific definition is to some degree self-defeating, but even this face-saving, somewhat superficial compromise took a long time to achieve. Therefore, the sanctions strategy will have to accept that much of the world will not see the Iran issue the same way, particularly in light of Iran's attacks on ISIS and other terrorist groups in Syria (alongside its support for Assad) and desire for stability in at least that part of the world. Even as the United States and its regional partners lament the reality that Iranian activities in Syria are self-interested to the extreme and in support of a brutal dictator, other countries will look to the end of this policy rather than the means and be satisfied (especially in a Europe that is challenged by an influx of refugees).

The most effective sanctions strategy would be one that accepts the low likelihood of global support and, therefore, the need for continued emphasis on U.S. unilateral measures that target particular bad actors in an evidence-based construct. Targeted sanctions that center on specific, provable connections between bad acts, bad actors, and Iran would be the hallmark of such a strategy, but spanning classes and types of foreign business entities. Banks, transportation firms, insurance agencies, and the like would all be on notice that the provision of support to U.S.-designated Iranian terrorist supporters and human rights violators would be a sanctionable offense. This, in turn, would maintain a substantial cost of doing business in Iran with an associated, negative effect on investment and trade. Iran's economy would not be devastated by such measures, which would largely mirror the U.S. strategy from 2006 to 2010. But Iran would find the situation uncomfortable and problematic, especially in the context of competition from other emerging markets. Iran would face some pressure internally to resolve the situation and, importantly, would see that its policies come with direct, clear costs. In fact, in comparison to a broader-brush sanctions campaign targeting Iranian oil because oil money pays for terrorism (or similar), this more targeted approach would be sellable to an international audience as well as translatable to an Iranian audience (even if that audience rejects some of the fundamental premises of such a strategy), and manageable for international businesses and banks (whose compliance functions would need to deal with the situation but as a business cost, rather than a complete hindrance). This strategy—reflected in the aforementioned bill passed in July 2017—calls for patience and perseverance, as well as the acknowledgment that, unlike with the nuclear program's rapid march toward provision of a fully fledged weapons capability, the nature of the Iranian threat is manageable in the intervening period.

One counterargument is that this strategy could conflict with the JCPOA at times. However, so long as the strategy does not result in a blanket sectoral approach, this complaint is based on an Iranian interpretation of the deal. The U.S. interpretation, which a plain reading of the text would support, is that the United States is entitled to continue enforcing its sanctions laws already on the books dealing with terrorism and human rights but not to engage in sector-wide, sweeping sanctions. The structure already exists; the explanation and basis for action has yet to be articulated.

This does not mean that there will not be times where the provisions of the JCPOA and this strategy conflict. One can easily imagine an Iranian bank for which sanctions were removed pursuant to the JCPOA being identified as having facilitated a transfer from Iran to a terrorist group, and then being sanctioned. But if the approach is evidence based, if it is methodical, if it is targeted rather than sectoral, and if it is clearly articulated, then both Iranian institutions will protect themselves from such problems and the international community will understand the strategy being executed. This may already be happening in some small ways. Iranian banks operating in the United Kingdom, for example, have started to identify entities and individuals in Iran with whom they will not do business in order to avoid this risk.[4] An Iranian banking initiative to cooperate with the Financial Action Task Force to similarly avoid risky banking relationships in Iran itself became intensely political in 2016, but was based on the same premise, ironically echoing the words of U.S. officials over the past decade: if Iran wants to engage in the international economy, it needs to adhere to its standards.[5]

Fourth, the United States and its partners should monitor the strategy's execution and continuously recalibrate their initial assumptions of Iranian resolve, the efficacy of the pain applied in shattering that resolve, and how best to improve the strategy. This is self-explanatory. However, it may take years to demonstrate real results given the constraints identified above.

Fifth, the United States and its partners should present Iran with a clear statement of the conditions necessary for the removal of pain, as well as offer to pursue any negotiations necessary to conclude an arrangement that removes the pain while satisfying U.S. and partner requirements.

Since the sanctions strategy outlined above is evidence- and conduct-based (rather than just "Iran" based), there are two straightforward ways for the sanctions regime to be removed: administratively, sanctions can be terminated if bad acts no longer take place or evidence is provided that casts doubt on the original sanctions; and diplomatically, in exchange for Iranian commitments that provide sufficient confidence to the United States and its partners that Iran will perform as it has promised.

Here, there will have to be a strong measure of vision on the part of the United States and its partners. Doubtless, some of those who opposed the JCPOA on the grounds that the United States could not accept an agreement with the present government of Iran, given its hostility and duplicity, will make a similar argument. They may suggest that the Iranians will never live up to a bargain and, in fact, that no bargain with Iran on such matters is enforceable or verifiable. However, this is inherently an issue that would arise in *any* agreement with the Iranians, whether through a negotiated settlement or an Iranian capitulation on the verge of regime economic and political collapse (which is unlikely to be realized in any event). Only through a reorganization of the Iranian government (read: regime change) can such a problem be avoided, and it would be an understatement to point out the difficulties and problems intrinsic to such an approach. Consequently, structuring an agreement will be an outcome of any such strategy; the considerations should instead be *how* to structure it and *under what circumstances might it be achievable*.

Regarding the first, a resulting agreement would require regional participation and support. Iran's support for terrorism is likely not because of a malevolent, nihilistic desire to destroy existing systems of government around the world. Rather, it is derived from a combination of interests, some of which may stem from its history as a revolutionary system and some of which stem from its own national security interests and needs. Fomenting unrest and revolution abroad can be about ideology; it can also be about defense in depth. Consequently, for Iran to agree to stop engaging in such activities, it will need a sense of assurance about its place in the region. Certainly, this also will be the prevailing demand of any regional parties that are prepared to countenance an arrangement with Tehran: they would want absolute, concrete assurances as to Iran's decision to no longer support such proxies.

An initial step, therefore, could be an exchange of assurances from all sides to respect the territorial integrity and political systems of their neighbors. Beyond serving as appropriate "diplo-speak" to begin a process, such an exchange of assurances would create a foundation for agreements on specific issues and measures necessary to execute an arrangement. After that, individual issues would need to be addressed, identifying acceptable levels and forms of support, compliance mechanisms, sanctions snap-back procedures, and the like to create a framework for Iran to stop engaging in regional bad acts and in exchange for specifically defined benefits. This diplomatic work would be time consuming and intensive, probably taking years to sort out.

Herein lies the major problem: the degree to which establishing the right international atmosphere for such negotiations will be complicated by real life. In the JCPOA negotiations, real-life problems associated with Iran's nuclear program, with Western sanctions, and even exogenous issues (like Ukraine) crept into the negotiating rooms and the context for the talks. JCPOA negotiators were able to work past these problems, in no small part because the multinational nature of the talks—with varying opinions across the table on these exogenous issues—created its own pressure for negotiators to keep their eyes on the ball. This may be much more difficult in a regional negotiation, particularly given the number of spoilers who may try to undermine progress in the talks. Terrorist attacks, military confrontations in the Persian Gulf, and even freak incidents of chance will all take place during negotiations around such a solution. Creating and maintaining the right environment for talks will be difficult, but—if they are to succeed—it will be necessary.

With respect to Iranian human rights, it is similarly possible to utilize a combination of sanctions and negotiations as a means of seeking improvements. Here, however, the most effective negotiating instrument may not be a regional arrangement, as there are widespread issues with human rights throughout the Middle East. Instead, human rights may be advanced further through negotiations and interactions between European and Iranian officials (who have maintained a human rights dialogue for over a decade) or through an incremental, stepwise process building on such tools as the Iranian bill of rights that was being advanced, as of this writing, by Iranian president Hassan Rouhani.

Sixth, the United States and its partners should accept the possibility that, notwithstanding a carefully crafted strategy, their efforts may fail. The United States and its partners must be prepared to acknowledge their failure and change course, or accept the risk that continuing with their present course could create worse outcomes in the long run.

As already noted, a sanctions strategy intended to achieve the identified objectives will face grave difficulties in the absence of an Iranian change of government (and it would be folly for the United States to attempt to engineer such a change given the long, bad history of U.S.-Iran relations). Given the complications involved in such an effort, the United States and its partners are better off trying to arrive at a mutually acceptable arrangement with Iran, using sanctions as the necessary source of leverage. But this effort may fail, either because it is an inherently difficult enterprise or because of exogenous factors. If it does fail, it will be necessary to instead focus on measures intended to limit the damage from Iran's provocative regional behavior (essentially, to put in place a firm containment strategy) or, in the case of human rights, intended to improve the living conditions of the average Iranian.

Russia in Ukraine

The Russian government and its core supporters in the Russian economy are under the most serious sanctions pressure still extant, save for North Korea. Moreover, the imposition of sanctions against Russia for its involvement in Ukrainian instability and acquisition of Crimea in 2014 also represents the most significant demonstration of coercive diplomatic pressure via sanctions in place as 2017 dawned. Aided and perhaps enabled by low oil prices, these sanctions have had a direct economic cost on Russia, measured by a drop in Russian GDP growth in 2014–2015, increased inflation, and currency depreciation. More intangibly, these sanctions have also created a negative impression of the Russian transition to democracy and its membership in the international community; its expulsion from the G-8 (which became once more the G-7 in 2014) was only the most visible manifestation of this shift.

Yet, the fundamental question remains: have the sanctions actually affected Russian behavior on the core topic of Ukraine and—if not—do they have any promise of doing so? In this, the Russia case is a prime example of the pain and resolve framework that I develop in this book. Moreover, even though Donald Trump may look to ease sanctions on Russia in his tenure (something Congress made more difficult with the legislation in July 2017), the case itself merits both study and examination insofar as our framework is concerned, given the significance of the problem being confronted and the country targeted.

Sanctions Approach Thus Far

The United States and the European Union began imposing sanctions against Russia in response to its activities in Ukraine in

March 2014, but the origins of the crisis go much farther back, arguably beginning with the collapse of the Soviet Union, when the independent state of Ukraine was formed. Within it, a social and cultural cleavage existed between the Russian-speaking east and Ukrainian-speaking west, which was only the most superficial demonstration of the much deeper difference between the regions. In 2013, these differences emerged in dramatic fashion, catalyzed by Ukraine's ongoing consideration of a deeper economic relationship with the European Union through a formal association agreement. This agreement had been under negotiation by the EU and Ukraine for many years leading up to 2013, and, although the negotiations were complicated and time consuming, by 2013 it appeared as if they would come to a conclusion.

In August 2013, the Russian government decided to make known its true feelings concerning the agreement and what it perceived to be a drift of Ukraine into the EU's sphere of influence (and, in a zero-sum frame, away from Russia). The Russians began subjecting imports from Ukraine to extra rigorous inspections, essentially slowing trade with Ukraine to a trickle. Russian officials implied that, should the Ukrainians proceed with their negotiations with the EU these requirements would become permanent. In 2013, Russia accounted for 25 percent of Ukraine's export market, helping to create the impression for Ukraine that to continue with the EU process would be—as a Russian government official made clear—"suicidal."[6]

Over the course of the fall of 2013, the Ukrainian government worked with the EU to identify ways in which the EU could compensate Ukraine for the loss of Russian trade. But, in its own show of economic force, the Russian government's pressure campaign was successful, leading then-Ukrainian President Viktor Yanukovych to back away from the negotiations with the EU.

However, the Russians may not have anticipated what impact this decision would have on internal Ukrainian politics. Protesters immediately began to congregate in Kyiv, angry about the decision to back away from the EU. Other protesters, these supportive of President Yanukovych and an orientation toward Moscow, arrived over time and there were to-be-expected clashes between them. In December 2013, after weeks of protests, Ukrainian police tried to clear protesters from the public spaces in Kyiv, most notably at Independence Square (known in Ukrainian as the Maidan). On December 17, the Russians sought to aid Yanukovych with an expansive economic package, lowering the price of Ukraine's natural gas import bill by a third and offering to buy $15 billion in Ukrainian debt.[7] But throughout January and February 2014, the situation deteriorated, with violence in the streets of Kyiv and—at the end of February—the collapse of the Ukrainian government. Yanukovych fled the country, leaving it in the hands of pro-Western groups who, in turn, decided to ban Russian as a second language and thus further inflamed eastern regions of Ukraine.

At the end of February, Crimea began to secede from Ukraine, requesting in March 2014 to join Russia instead. The Russian government accepted its request and absorbed Crimea formally on March 18. Unrest and violence then spread throughout eastern Ukraine, spurred on by the emergence of pro-Russian militia groups widely believed to include Russian military personnel, although the Russian government has dismissed the claim.

The United States and the European Union responded by imposing sanctions against Russian and Ukrainian individuals and entities believed to be involved in the violence in eastern Ukraine as well as the seizure of Crimea. Sanctions also were imposed that limit cooperation with Russia in defense areas. By September 2014, the United States and EU had expanded their sanctions to cover additional sectors of the Russian economy, including measures that:

- Prohibit providing new debt or new equity greater than thirty days' maturity to identified persons operating in the Russian financial sector.

- Prohibit providing new debt greater than ninety days' maturity to identified persons operating in the Russian energy sector.
- Prohibit the export of goods, services (except for financial services), or technology in support of exploration or production for deepwater, Arctic offshore, or shale projects that have the potential to produce oil in Russia, to identified persons operating in the Russian energy sector.
- Prohibit providing new debt greater than thirty days' maturity to identified persons operating in the Russian defense sector.
- Impose sanctions on persons operating in Russia's defense sector.[8]

These sanctions were principally intended to impose economic costs on Russia by forcing the Russians to find sources of financing for their oil and gas sector projects other than American or European banks and investors. In a normal world, the most likely alternative source would be domestic financing. However, these sanctions were imposed amid a collapse in international oil prices throughout the summer and fall of 2014. From a high point of $115.19 per barrel (Brent) on June 19, 2014, the price fell by 52 percent to $55.27 per barrel (Brent) to close out the year.[9] And, with it, Russian export revenues also fell. Russian president Vladimir Putin noted in April 2015 that lost oil sales cost Russia $160 billion and put a significant dent in the $350 billion that Russia had grown accustomed to earning each year through energy exports.[10] That said, the Russian economy also has a tradition of trimming imports in order to manage export shortfalls, something that the Russian government intentionally triggered when it imposed its own sanctions on Europe covering mainly agricultural goods. As I have separately noted, the Russian economy shed itself of roughly the equivalent in import costs as its lost export revenue in 2014, helping to avoid contributing to its hard-currency crisis and ruble depreciation that began in fall 2014 and continued into early 2015.[11]

Still, by early 2015, the Russian economy was in poor shape, with much of Russia's foreign currency reserves being spent in an attempt to settle its foreign debts. This pressure has presented challenges to key stakeholders of the Russian economy, such as Vnesheconombank, which required an $18 billion bailout in December 2015.[12] Continued weak oil prices and the absence of sanctions relief—which some in the market had unwisely assumed would be quickly forthcoming—have amplified the damage already.[13] As of June 2017, the United States continued to maintain its sanctions lists, updating them periodically and harmonizing them with EU lists. As noted, the U.S. Congress passed legislation in July 2017 that, inter alia, expanded the prohibitions on U.S. persons regarding additional oil and gas projects and other activities involving Russia. Though questions remain about the Trump administration's enforcement as of this writing, the signal sent is of continued readiness to impose pressure. The practical effect has been to demonstrate to the Russians that, absent political progress in Ukraine, the sanctions will continue to bite and be ratcheted up albeit modestly.

Faced with such pressure, the Russians, Ukrainians, and Europeans have engaged in two rounds of negotiations intended to resolve the situation, each beginning with a cease-fire. The first such arrangement—called "Minsk 1"—collapsed shortly after it was concluded in September 2014. Minsk 2, reached in February 2015, has been subject to almost daily violations, with the cease-fire being broken on countless occasions. Similarly, the political process required in Minsk 2 in Kyiv also suffers from the Ukrainian government's incoherent politics and internal disputes. As of this writing, the deadlines for the Minsk 2 political processes have been extended but show no signs of being met. Rather than moving the conflict from its frozen status, it seems likely that sanctions will continue to be in place against Russia for the long term.

Applying Our Model

The case of Russia and Ukraine offers an opportunity to assess the sanctions framework in a live case, with the possibility of adjustments still to be made. *First, we must identify objectives for the imposition of pain and define minimum necessary remedial steps that Russia must take for pain to be removed.* From the start of the sanctions campaign, U.S. officials have emphasized that sanctions are intended to deal with Russian intervention throughout Ukraine, the pressure applied on the government in Kyiv, and what the United States considers to be the illegal annexation of Crimea. President Obama made this point clear when he first decided to impose sanctions on Russia in March 2014.[14] But there have been questions about precisely what Russia would have to do to reverse the sanctions.

Initially, U.S. and European official statements were ambiguous and somewhat contradictory on how sanctions would be reversed. But by early 2016, the United States and European officials had clarified that the bulk of the sanctions imposed against Russia would be relieved if the terms of Minsk 2 were fully implemented, while sanctions that specifically targeted Russian occupation of Crimea (essentially a series of specific designations of individual Russians and Ukrainians) would remain in place so long as Crimea remained in Russian hands. Though the Trump administration has offered some contradictory views, it has generally maintained this position, which Congress also reaffirmed in its July 2017 legislation. Assuming this remains the case, Russia has therefore been presented with a reasonably clear picture.

Second, we should understand as much as possible Russia's vulnerabilities, interests, commitment to interference in Ukrainian sovereignty, and readiness to absorb pain. From the perspective of effectively targeting the Russian economy's vulnerability, the sanctions campaign has been a strong success. Sanctioners displayed considerable sophistication in their identification of Russian economic weaknesses and potential points of leverage, particularly in changing the terms of Russia's ability to manage its external debt. Understanding this weakness permitted the United States and European Union to apply fairly precise pressure on the Russian economy without imperiling its ability and willingness to supply Europe with natural gas and avoid broader economic collapse. Pressure and pain were created, with a sense of future economic menace to come should outside demands fail to be met. Luck and timing no doubt played a role: had the sanctions against Russia taken place in the context of $100 per barrel of oil, as opposed to during an oil price collapse, then the effects would have been far less damaging for the Russians. However, even with good timing, proper sanctions design played a major role and, though existing debt has become less of a significant vulnerability, Russia's need for foreign financing and reliance on oil and gas exports remain viable targets for sanctions pressure. The new sanctions legislation adopted by Congress in July 2017 seeks to capitalize on these vulnerabilities by further reducing the incentive to do business in Russia's oil and gas sector, to engage in joint venture partnerships that give Russia technical knowledge it needs, and ostracize its markets from the outside. It also foreshadows new sanctions to come, including potentially on Russian sovereign bonds that could imperil future growth.

That said, the sanctions campaign has fallen short of a complete understanding of Russian national values and readiness to absorb costs, particularly with respect to Crimea. The sanctions regime has yet to acknowledge that Russia is fully prepared to absorb considerable pain in order to maintain control of Crimea. As noted above, the sanctions regime itself has become differentiated around eastern Ukraine and Crimea, but nonetheless, the degree to which Crimea would serve as a "bloody shirt" cause for the Russian public (and thereby a strengthener of resolve) was not registered fully in the announcement of sanctions against Russia.

Third, we should develop a strategy to carefully, methodically, and efficiently increase pain on those areas that are vulnerabilities while avoiding those which are not. Thus far, the sanctions regime has shown patience in its imposition of pain on Russia. This patience is not entirely strategic, as there is countervailing pressure from Europe to refrain from imposing even tougher sanctions that could further undermine still legitimate trade between Europe and Russia. The Trump administration's haphazard approach to Russia has also devalued expectations for sanctions contribution to the overall strategy, as open questions exist about its enforcement posture. Still, the expectation in the market increasingly appears resigned to some new pressure, even if foisted upon Europe and Trump by the U.S. Congress.

However, as noted above, sanctioners may have let too much pressure off already. From this perspective, the careful, methodical, and efficient increase in pressure on Russia has flagged, undermining the crucial momentum needed to translate political concern into political concession. To be sure, there have been some incremental improvements in the sanctions regime, with some additional targets being added to lists over the course of 2015–2017. However, the result is still that while sanctions have not been eased, the momentum behind them has. Anecdotally, the only change that I experienced myself on a December 2016 trip to Moscow is that quality parmesan cheese was no longer available at restaurants, hardly a level of pain that inspires a desire to throw off the sanctions regime through negotiations. Systemically, Russia is still under strain. But it is harder to translate that sense of economic pressure into policy change absent more tangible illustrations of pain. Obviously, this should be reversed, with consideration of additional sanctions designations going hand in hand with the imposition of stiffer penalties for the Russian economy the longer that the crisis goes on. Russia has adapted to the pressure in place. Even if new forms of pressure seem modest, Russia should not be permitted to obtain de facto sanctions relief simply by virtue of having outlasted the pressure being applied. Sanctions adopted in July 2017 are a start, but additional measures—perhaps targeting other aspects of the Russian economy beyond oil and gas, such as its ability to generate international investment in its sovereign debt—should be considered, particularly as part of a broader European-U.S. endeavor and enlisting the aid and support of other partners around the world (such as Japan).

Fourth, we must monitor the execution of the strategy and continuously recalibrate its initial assumptions of Russian resolve, the efficacy of the pain applied in shattering that resolve, and how best to improve the strategy. Many people within the U.S. government and European partner governments are monitoring the implementation of sanctions. I will take on faith the likelihood that those responsible for sanctions imposition are seeing momentum dwindling and sanctions drift in the measures applied thus far. But, as noted, this has yet to translate into the "recalibration" and intensification necessary to change Russian resolve.

While the United States and EU remain entrenched in their view that Russia must relinquish its control over Crimea, there is no indication Russia is remotely prepared to concede this point. Russia has incorporated Crimea into its own state structures and considers the territory to be part of Russia proper now. People living in Crimea have expressed readiness to remain part of Russia, at least according to polling data.[15] And the text of Minsk 2 would—at least if read literally—seem to accept that Crimea is to be treated as a wholly separate matter from the need to address Russian interference in eastern Ukraine, as the word is not even mentioned in the text of the Minsk 2 agreement.[16] It is likely that Russia would not have signed on to Minsk 2, for all its flaws, without some indemnification of its control over Crimea and U.S. and European rhetoric since Minsk 2 bears out acceptance of this concept, albeit with the proviso that some Russian and Ukrainian individuals would remain under sanctions specifically tied to the annexation of Crimea until that situation is remedied.

Recession, inflation, and shortages of goods are important indicators of the economic stress being felt by common Russians, and the threat to the solvency and integrity of the financial system are a manifestation of similar problems for the wealthy elite. But other measures, the Russian government continues to do well at home. According to the Levada Center (a Russian nongovernmental organization that conducts polling in Russia), Putin enjoyed an 85 percent popularity rating in December 2015, which has been fairly consistent since he experienced a meteoric rise in February–March 2014.[17] Even taking into account the possibility that polling data may be subject to either direct or latent manipulation, there is scant evidence that Putin has lost the support of the Russian people despite their economic problems. As a consequence, although economic pain has been borne, it is difficult to argue that it has translated into real pressure on Putin to change course rather than to find ways to deal with the problems created by sanctions in other ways.

In this regard, the Russians have been active in seeking out new markets for their energy exports and financing that do not rely on the United States or Europe. In December 2015, Russia announced its intention to issue its first sovereign bond in Chinese renminbi, expected to be worth approximately $1 billion; this follows similar actions undertaken by private Russian banks since 2013.[18] There have also been reports that Russia and China are working together on a natural gas trading relationship that could be worth $400 billion.[19] Russian strategy is to manage the problem by seeking to neuter the sanctions rather than to accommodate the concerns of the United States or Europe. Russian interest in the candidacy of Donald Trump is a subject beyond the focus of this book, but countering U.S. sanctions pressure may have played a part in Russia's thinking in this regard. The Russians have also sought to prevent the acceleration of sanctions, reaching out to European governments (particularly those that might be persuaded to break the EU consensus required to extend sanctions) and—arguably—agreeing to cooperate with cease-fire arrangements as a way of sucking wind from the sails of those in Europe and the United States that were seeking expanded sanctions. Russia has been aided in this regard by the persistent fears of some in Europe that, if sanctions were to be ratcheted up too far, Russia could respond by cutting the export of natural gas sales to Europe, even though doing so would damage Russian economic interests dramatically. From a pain/resolve perspective, Russian resolve therefore appears—at least on the surface—to be fairly strong.

Fifth, we should present Russia with a clear statement of the conditions necessary for the removal of pain, as well as an offer to pursue any negotiations necessary to conclude an arrangement that removes the pain while satisfying U.S. and European requirements.

Russia has been given a clear signal as to what it must do for sanctions to be removed, with negotiations serving to underscore the necessary nature of a possible quid pro quo. The unresolved question remains the nature of the sanctioning states' requirements. In the United States and the EU as a whole, there remains a persistent sense that full restoration of pre-2013 Ukrainian sovereignty is an indivisible aim. However, press reports continue to emerge that others in Europe may have a different sense of what is necessary. As suggested above, this is not necessarily a bad thing, if Russian resistance to at least the Crimea-related part of the crisis would otherwise make diplomatic progress unattainable. However, insofar as offering *clarity* is concerned, the mixed messages coming from Europe and within the United States are, at best, confusing to Moscow.

Sixth, the United States and its partners should accept the possibility that, notwithstanding a carefully crafted strategy, their efforts may fail because of inherent inefficiencies in the strategy, a misunderstanding of the target, or an exogenous boost in Russia's resolve and capacity to resist. Either way, the United States and its partners must be prepared to either acknowledge their failure and change course or accept the risk that continuing with their present course could create worse outcomes in the long run.

As has been suggested above, U.S. and European sanctions efforts may have been coming to this point even before the election of Donald Trump. Consideration with Ukrainian officials is now necessary to see whether a resolution of the crisis that protects Ukrainian sovereignty (and that of other Eastern European states) is possible and in what form, followed by consultation with the Russians about potential acceptable end states for the sanctions campaign, especially if Trump is inclined to cancel it regardless.

This conclusion also lends itself to another general point about sanctions: even if sanctions objectives shift, they must not shift without accommodation. Even if the United States did not accept the annexation of Crimea, the situation on the ground in Ukraine, the contents of Minsk 2, and the necessity of maintaining a united front with Europe mean that—for all practical purposes—the annexation has been ceded to the Russians. That may be, in the end, for the best if it resolves one of Russia's long-simmering frustrations with Ukraine. But from a sanctions pain/resolve calculus, the ceding of Crimea's annexation—the reversal of which was a core objective of the sanctions regime—would be highly damaging unless the sanctions regime is itself adjusted to acknowledge the concession. It creates both unclear thresholds for the sanctions target, as well as the potential for misunderstanding the sanctioning state's leadership. Clarity of purpose and communication of it to all sides is imperative for sanctions to work as intended. For this reason, the clarity given by U.S. and European officials in early 2016 as to the scope of Ukraine-related sanctions has been helpful in addressing this potential risk.

Democratic People's Republic of Korea (North Korea)

The Democratic People's Republic of Korea (DPRK, or North Korea, as it is colloquially known) has been effectively an international outlaw since it came into existence in the aftermath of the

Second World War. As a client state of the Soviet Union and China during the Cold War, North Korea was isolated from the Western bloc to a significant degree. However, even in this context, its activities were often strange, provocative, and dangerous. For example, North Korea engaged in extensive kidnapping operations starting in the 1940s and continuing through at least the 1970s, intended to bring in a combination of intellectuals, sources of intelligence, and cultural information for North Korean exploitation.[20] Throughout the Cold War, North Korean intelligence officers and special forces infiltrated South Korea using carefully dug tunnels under the Demilitarized Zone (DMZ); some of these tunnels would have permitted a covert invasion of the South, with thousands of DPRK troops theoretically able to pass through them hourly.[21] North Korea's seizure of the U.S.S. *Pueblo* in 1968 raised significant tensions between the United States and North Korea, and sparked discussion of contingency plans that—ultimately—could have led to a resumption of the Korean War.[22] In this context, North Korea's actions since the end of the Cold War, particularly its program to obtain nuclear weapons and subsequent testing of them (as well as long range ballistic missiles), are largely in keeping with a history of taking steps that many other countries would pursue only reluctantly. They point to a regime that remains a threat to its neighborhood and to international security and stability more generally.

Sanctions Approach Thus Far

The international community has responded to North Korea's actions, specifically its nuclear and missile programs, primarily by the application of UN sanctions against the country. Starting with UNSCR 1718 in October 2006, the UN Security Council (UNSC) forbade trade with North Korea in nuclear and missile-related goods and imposed targeted financial sanctions on a list of individuals and entities that—as of June 2017—now includes fifty-three individuals and forty-six entities of various importance to North Korea's government and military.[23] The sanctions have also expanded to address different aspects of the North Korean economy, including its primary export industry—coal extraction—and its broader links to the international economy. As of December 2016, it is against UNSC sanctions to permit unfettered DPRK diplomatic activity in UN member states; obligatory to inspect DPRK-bound or outbound cargo; and to provide a range of financial and related services to North Korea or its constituent elements.

National governments have also responded with their own sanctions regimes. The United States steadily added to its national sanctions program, culminating with a comprehensive embargo against North Korea in March 2016 and building on decades of a diverse array of more specific prohibitions. South Korea and Japan have similar sanctions regimes and have in recent years been more willing to apply pressure on other countries that continue to do business with North Korea. In December 2016, for example, Japan prohibited ships from entering its ports that previously entered North Korean ports, regardless of their flag or origin.[24] South Korea's economic interactions with the North have long been modest (limited to a joint venture at Kaesong that is periodically opened and closed with the prevailing political winds), but the South Koreans—especially under President Park—have sought to improve economic and political ties with China in order to convince the Chinese to switch or at least temper their relationship with the Korean Peninsula. South Korea's willingness to accept the deployment of U.S. theater missile defenses in 2016 was, in part, a way of applying pressure on China to change its approach, though China's hostile reaction may show some of the limitations and risks inherent in this effort.[25] European and other likeminded partners have similarly sought to apply pressure on North Korea, and the likeminded campaign has included trips around the world to third-party governments to discourage military and economic cooperation with the DPRK.[26]

All of these steps are naturally intended to increase the pain on North Korea such that it would agree to modify its behavior. Notably, there have been some individual indications of success on this front. For example, in Juan Zarate's book *Treasury's War*, he recounts the case of Banco Delta Asia (BDA), which was found in 2005 to be in possession of approximately $25 million of the Kim family's personal funds. The September 2005 imposition of sanctions against these funds touched a nerve with North Korea, and ultimately may have contributed to North Korea's willingness to negotiate an agreement with the United States and other countries in the "Six Party Talks," composed of China, Japan, North Korea, Russia, South Korea, and the United States, that led to the dismantlement and inspection of North Korean nuclear facilities in 2007.[27] An earlier Chinese cut-off of heating oil also has been credited by some as helping bring North Korea to the Six Party Talks in the first place, though an examination of the chronology of North Korean nuclear and missile activities would suggest such pain was insufficient to moderate North Korea's actual activities of concern.[28]

Of course, this is the rub: while sanctions pressure has built on North Korea, so too has pressure built on the outside world. Since 2005, North Korea has tested nuclear weapons five times. North Korea has claimed that its tests have helped it improve its designs and has boasted of even testing thermonuclear weapons (which are both more efficient in terms of material usage and more destructive). Though there is some reasonable skepticism that North Korea has achieved this level of technical sophistication, it is not impossible.[29] Nor is it impossible that North Korea has perfected a missile-deployable nuclear warhead, one that is considered sufficiently "standardized" to be reproducible at North Korean will.[30] With such technical developments, North Korea has not only demonstrated physical capacities that it can utilize to threaten and even attack its adversaries, perhaps as far away as the West Coast of the United States at some point in the near future. North Korea has also demonstrated considerable resolve in the face of Western and even Chinese concerted pressure.

To what end remains an open question. Based on reports from various non-governmental sources, it is possible that the North Koreans are interested in bartering their nuclear weapons capabilities for a peace treaty with the United States, removal of U.S. troops from South Korea, and support in fixing its ailing economy.[31] It is also possible that North Korea has no intention of abandoning its nuclear or missile programs and is merely setting the context for its future treatment. Conscious of the historical legacy of dictators who set aside their weapons of mass destruction programs (Muammar Qaddhafi) or had them set aside involuntarily (Bashar al-Assad and Saddam Hussein), Kim Jong Un may believe that nuclear weapons and ballistic missiles are now permanent features of his regime, preserving it from external attack.

The United States has made a consistent policy decision—from Bill Clinton through Donald Trump—to oppose North Korea's possession of nuclear weapons. Likewise, Congress has sown a consistent readiness to impose costs on North Korea for its behavior and to adopt ever more stringent sanctions. Consequently, it is likely that sanctions will continue to figure in the U.S. strategy going forward.

Applying Our Model

The obvious question is: sanctions to what end? Applying our framework can give some indication of what is possible and what is necessary.

First, we must identify objectives for the imposition of pain and define minimum necessary remedial steps that North Korea must take for pain to be removed. Here, it is easier to identify an objective for pain imposition than it is to define the minimum necessary remedial steps North Korea must take. This is because a decision about how far the North must go ultimately revolves around the U.S. expectation for North Korea's future political and military development.

On its face, the U.S. objective and required minimum steps from North Korea overlap: the United States wishes North Korea to abandon its nuclear weapons and ballistic missile programs, submitting them to international verification. South Korea, Japan, and other interested states share this ambition. It is consistent with the 2005 Joint Statement of the Six Party Talks, in which North Korea "committed to abandoning all nuclear weapons and existing nuclear programs and returning, at an early date, to the Treaty on the Nonproliferation of Nuclear Weapons and to IAEA safeguards."[32] It is also consistent with the 1992 Joint Statement on the Denuclearization of the Korean Peninsula, issued by North and South Korea, at least insofar as the nuclear program is concerned. North Korea's ballistic missile program is in a somewhat more ambiguous position, although repeated UNSC resolutions have forbidden North Korea from testing ballistic missiles. However, the key point remains: unless it is willing to change policy substantially, the United States has very little by way of a fallback position, particularly given the long and checkered history of North Korean "freeze" and other suspensions arrangements.

Herein lies one of the problems surrounding the North Korean nuclear issue: North Korea has also not indicated a readiness to abandon its missile or nuclear programs. In fact, in the 2005 Joint Statement, "the DPRK stated that it has the right to peaceful uses of nuclear energy. The other parties expressed their respect and agreed to discuss, at an appropriate time, the subject of the provision of light water reactor to the DPRK."[33] From this perspective, a floor has been established with respect to how far North Korea might go and, as with the Iran and Russia cases, an expectation that comes with diplomacy and sanctions that the end result will be a managed and monitored North Korean nuclear program rather than elimination. Persuading North Korea to accept some constraints on its missile program is probably essential, given its provocative nature and the criticism that the Iran JCPOA met for not addressing this problem.

Second, we should understand as much as possible North Korea's vulnerabilities, interests, commitment to its nuclear and missile programs, and readiness to absorb pain. We do know much about North Korea's countrywide vulnerabilities. Experts can wax on about the nature of the North Korean political system and economy, for even though sources of information are few, there are enough to draw a decent picture of how the system operates. Such vulnerabilities may or may not be significant in the unique case of North Korea because of its extreme domination by the ruling clique. North Korea's leadership has shown a steadfast unwillingness to consider the interests of its population, with only a select, isolated clique bearing most of the fruits of North Korean labor. Under Kim Jong Un (and, to a lesser extent, his father, Kim Jong Il), this has started to change and there have been indications of increased market-based economic activity.[34] But as of yet, we still have little indication that the fundamentals of the North Korean economy or the political treatment of the working class will improve to any great degree.

Because of this, North Korea presents a different target picture to the international community than either the Iranian or Russian cases. In this way, North Korea has shown some of the same qualities as Saddam Hussein, prepared to absorb pain as a national matter because the North Korean government merely passes it along to the population. The North Korean government has shown considerable resolve in defense of its nuclear and missile programs. Taken in combination, this suggests a regime that is largely insensate to the pain being applied by the outside world and fully prepared to take its nuclear and missile interests to the mat.

On the other hand, we also have some experience with North Korean reactions to external pressure, as the BDA case in particular demonstrates. The question is therefore less about whether the North Korean regime can and will feel pressure and more about ensuring that it is the right pressure, at the right time, and for the right reasons. From this perspective, the imperative is not to identify national vulnerabilities per se but rather regime vulnerabilities (and even personal vulnerabilities for the country's major players). In one sense, this may be an easier task than targeting an entire country, where there may be myriad viewpoints to balance. On the other hand, missing the essential target's vulnerability also means that any pressure applied is likely to be ineffective at best.

It also may mean than the North Korea's vulnerability might derive from lost opportunities for the future rather than from current pain. As long as North Korea proceeds in its current manner, it will continue to be an international pariah. This may be broadly acceptable to many in the ruling establishment, but perhaps not to Kim Jong Un who has displayed considerable interest in his country being seen as modern even with respect to superficial things, such as his decision to build facilities that are the equivalent to those being constructed for the upcoming Winter Olympic Games in South Korea. This is not to say that Kim Jong Un could be convinced to give up his nuclear and missile capabilities for the price of hosting international sports competitions! But we would be imprudent to dismiss any potential factors in developing a picture of the pressures and incentives that might be brought to bear in both a negotiation and in a sanctions strategy, particularly when the actual target of pressure is—in many ways—a single individual in Pyongyang.

Third, we should develop a strategy to carefully, methodically, and efficiently increase pain on those areas that are vulnerabilities, while avoiding those which are not. With our understanding of North Korea from the second element of our framework, we can now formulate a strategy that applies judicious, timely pressure on the North Koreans. Rather than simply adopting sanctions in a tit-for-tat manner, which has typified the U.S. reaction to North

Korea over two presidential administrations, the Trump team should set the terms of the debate with a comprehensive approach that contains an offer to the North Koreans and a commitment on how sanctions would be applied.

First and foremost, this strategy would begin with an offer to talk in private, rather than the imposition of sanctions. Trump's team should hear out the North Korean negotiators and formulate on the basis of those talks a precise picture of how the North Koreans see a possible resolution, what the North Koreans can concede, and in exchange for what. Almost certainly, this will represent an ideal outcome for North Korea rather than its bottom line, but the contours of North Korea's final needs will likely be present, if obscured with additional demands.

Assuming that the North Koreans have a remotely reasonable end state in mind, the United States can then formulate a set of reciprocal steps that it would be prepared to take, as well as a sense of bottom lines. For example, it is unrealistic to expect reunification of the Koreas as part of any initial deal and, consequently, for the United States to offer the removal of U.S. troops from the peninsula as part of an agreement at this stage. However, there are lower-level steps that might be taken by both sides that could reduce tensions (such as a halt in missile tests and large-scale military exercises). From here, other, deeper, and more significant steps could be discussed.

In the meantime, the United States should also present to the North Koreans a clear picture of the consequences for a failure of talks. This would include not only sanctions but also specific pressure brought to bear on the finances and external activities of North Korean elites. This is fully in keeping with the current U.S. (and UNSC) strategy. What's missing is a clear sense of cooperation from China and willingness to apply sustained pressure on the North for its failure to come to terms. This may be changing, as noted above, and as late as April 2017, the Chinese demonstrated increased commitment in this regard by banning coal purchases from North Korea altogether. (It is also possible that this issue will be swept up in the interplay of the Trump administration and Chinese government, particularly as other issues—such as the future of the South China Sea—remain unsettled.) The United States should lay out to China in stark terms its willingness to work together toward a diplomatic arrangement and even to consider concessions that were not previously on the table (such as on military exercises). But the United States should further communicate its expectation that China will also play a part and that the consequences of having failed to do so could include—among other things—a continued U.S. strategic build-up in the region that may create insecurity in China. Sanctions against Chinese institutions can and should be considered, where necessary, but the key threat in China's consideration with respect to North Korea is less business and more the threat of instability on the Korean Peninsula (with refugees potentially pouring across its borders) or reunification on South Korean (and U.S.) terms bring U.S. forces to the Yalu River. China must be presented with the unenviable, but necessary, choice between the best of two evils in its attempts to ward off instability and crisis, preferably to apply pressure on North Korea to seek a resolution of the nuclear and missile crisis and reduction of tensions. And, of course, such a sanctions regime will require sustained cooperation from non-Chinese foreign parties.

In the meantime, of course, the sanctions regime in place can and should continue to function with respect to depriving North Korea of the items it requires to develop and sustain its nuclear and missile programs (if any such items still must be imported), as well as to prevent North Korea from exporting arms and providing technical support to arms recipients. As the UNSC POE's report on North Korea issued on February 27, 2017, makes clear, North Korea has continued these activities notwithstanding UNSC sanctions and needs only a few successes to derive the kind of hard currency income necessary to prop up the regime in Pyongyang.

Preventing these transfers and deals ought to remain a priority while talks proceed.

Fourth, we must monitor the execution of the strategy and continuously recalibrate its initial assumptions of North Korean resolve, the efficacy of the pain applied in shattering that resolve, and how best to improve the strategy. As with previous sections, this step requires little elaboration.

Fifth, we should present North Korea with a clear statement of the conditions necessary for the removal of pain and offer to pursue any negotiations necessary to arrive at an arrangement that removes the pain while satisfying U.S. and partner country requirements. As noted above, and perhaps distinct from other sanctions efforts presently ongoing, this must be an intrinsic element of the sanctions strategy as well, given North Korea's limited appreciation for the nature of its economic vulnerabilities and the needs of its captive population.

Sixth, the United States and its partners should accept the possibility that, notwithstanding a carefully crafted strategy, their efforts may fail because of either inherent inefficiencies in the strategy, a misunderstanding of the target, or an exogenous boost in North Korea's resolve and capacity to resist. Either way, the United States and its partners must be prepared to acknowledge their failure and change course or else accept the risk that continuing with the present course could create worse outcomes in the long run.

Although this element of the framework is phrased as a possibility, it may be more reasonably stated as the most probable outcome of a sanctions campaign that does not involve or does not achieve a diplomatic settlement of the situation. North Korea's readiness to absorb pain in the surety that its leadership can survive and its population remains expendable undermines the utility of a sanctions-primacy approach. For this reason, the suggested strategy places further diplomacy at the center of the effort, with an expectation that—should it fail—the U.S. strategy would likely revert to an even more aggressive "containment" posture that seeks to mitigate the worst of North Korea's threats (through nuclear deterrence and missile defense), prevent proliferation (through expanded interdiction authorities), and assist the North Korean population in the event of regime collapse.

In this regard, North Korea demonstrates a central theme of this book: that sanctions are ultimately a tool of leverage, no more and no less. Leverage can help achieve solutions, but only if solutions actually exist. In the end, the effectiveness of sanctions as a tool is only so good as the integrity of the policy in question and the readiness of the country targeted to respond to the pressure applied.

Conclusion

THIS BOOK BEGAN WITH a reminder of how much sanctions, for all their involvement in statecraft throughout history, have changed in the past century. This observation flows from an understanding of the ways in which sanctions tools, the means of their application, and the substantive rationale for their use have all changed in modern times. The cases discussed in this book—and Iran in particular—all bear out this assertion, particularly when the details of the tools selected are considered. Who in 432 BCE Athens would have imagined a sanctions regime based upon the number of days that a foreign country's firms could have to repay their debts to banks thousands of miles away? Moreover, who in 432 BCE Athens would have imagined that such a sanctions regime could take place while one of its architects—in this case, U.S. Secretary of State John Kerry—sat with the foreign minister of the sanctions target—Sergey Lavrov—in conference rooms throughout Europe to deal with international crises on such issues as the Middle East and climate change? The world is a different place than it was in 432 BCE, and the lessons we take from the tools used then, as opposed to now, are different.

But the reason sanctions scholars appeal to the Peloponnesian War in beginning their surveys of sanctions is because such a grounding helps to underscore the degree to which people have not changed, nor their basic motivations and desires, an idea I explore in this book. Pain set against resolve, coupled with elements of human nature and existence, helps draw the connection between interests, actions, and decisions of cultures and governments the world over. And the comparison is made without having to resort to what one author has described as the "methodological gimmickry" of policy analysis, in this case a mathematical abstraction of the dynamics evaluated in this book.[1] Rather, this book sought to elaborate a way of evaluating sanctions and designing them for maximum effect, drawing on common considerations of basic interests, mindsets, and values, leaving to the individual sanctions program and its analysts the task of defining what is worth inclusion in the model for particular countries and problems.

The result is, for policymakers, a six-element process for developing a case-by-case approach for the imposition of sanctions within the general framework of influencing resolve with pressure:

- *Identify objectives for the imposition of pain and define minimum necessary remedial steps that the target state must take for pain to be removed.* This must be done with rigor and clarity, especially with regard to the conditions under which victory can be considered "achieved." It is worse than useless to define a sanctions regime without specific objectives, and the same applies to the creation of an analytical structure for assessing the efficacy of sanctions measures. For our purposes, defining victory conditions also permits analysis of the opponent's resolve levels for both the desired end result as well as other interests. Importantly, at this stage, it is not necessary to

communicate these minimum necessary steps to the sanctioned state: for tactical reasons involving negotiations,
they may never be disclosed. But the sanctioning state
itself must know the answer.

- *Understand as much as possible the nature of the target,
  including its vulnerabilities, interests, commitment to whatever it did to prompt sanctions, and readiness to absorb
  pain.* This requires a deep, rigorous analysis of the target
  state, defining its key national priorities with as much clarity as possible. They should be ranked in order, although
  the separation of the ranks may be artificial. The point is
  not to define a mathematically precise sequence of interests
  but rather to understand where the object of the sanctions
  policy falls in the hierarchy. In this way, the imposition of
  sanctions can be pursued with an understanding of how
  heavy a lift will be needed. To develop this construct, it is
  useful to have as comprehensive an understanding of the
  country's history and culture as possible, as well as to avoid
  facile overstatements about the importance of one priority
  over another. Particular care must be taken to avoid mirror
  imaging, in particular, and the assumption that the sanctions target thinks about problems in the same fashion as
  the sanctioner.
- *Develop a strategy to carefully, methodically, and efficiently
  increase pain on those areas that are vulnerabilities while
  avoiding those that are not.* It is prudent for policymakers to define for themselves the degree to which they are
  prepared to impose pain on their adversary and those
  who cooperate with it to prevail over the sanctioned state.
  Policymakers should know, in advance, whether they are
  prepared to bankrupt their adversary, sending its population into penury or not. They do not necessarily need to
  act upon this information in the first instance, but they
  must be aware of how far they are prepared to go in order

to design effective sanctions and to avoid undermining their own expressions of resolve by—for example—ruling out those sanctions approaches that could cause excessive humanitarian consequences in the sanctioned country. Policymakers need not even acknowledge any limits to their sanctions policies, but they must know those limits and have absolute clarity as to the degree to which the underlying challenge must be confronted. Resolve by the sanctioning state and understanding the resolve of the adversary are equally essential to success. For the purposes of our analysis, however, this information serves another purpose: helping to structure the arcs of available pain and pressure.

- *Monitor the execution of the strategy and continuously recalibrate its initial assumptions of target state resolve, the efficacy of the pain applied in shattering that resolve, and how best to improve the strategy.* This must begin with the assembly of key facts about the various resolve elements and form a picture of how changes to those elements can be measured as sanctions pressure is applied.

- *Present the target state with a clear statement of the conditions necessary for the removal of pain, as well as an offer to pursue any negotiations necessary to conclude an arrangement that removes the pain while satisfying the sanctioning state's requirements.* As noted with respect to Iran, any sanctions regime adopted in order to achieve a diplomatic solution and not merely for the sadistic application of pain will, at some point, require this kind of conversation with the sanctions target. For sanctions to have proper, positive leverage and to play a role in getting to that solution, the sanctioning state must be clear in its communications with the sanctions target, explaining the why of sanctions and the how of sanctions removal.

- *Accept the possibility that, notwithstanding a carefully crafted strategy, the sanctioning state may fail because of inherent inefficiencies in the strategy, a misunderstanding of the target, or an exogenous boost in the target's resolve and capacity to resist. Either way, a state must be prepared either to acknowledge its failure and change its course, or to accept the risk that continuing with its present course could create worse outcomes in the long run.* This stage could accompany any framework for a national security or foreign policy task. But it is particularly and uniquely appropriate and necessary for discussion of sanctions. As the Iraq case demonstrates, sanctions have—in the past—become "fire and forget" weapons that are expected to continue achieving results. Moreover, if and when the underlying policy associated with sanctions fails, the instrument itself often gets the blame. Not only is this a harmful way of conducting policy analysis but it also may be a cause of worse conflicts in the long run (as, again, Iraq in 2003 shows). A state would not undertake a war without constantly evaluating the costs and benefits, nor would a state do so with regard to normal diplomatic activity. Sanctions should be treated in the same fashion.

In the end, sanctions developers can think of their work as creating a complex maze into which they intend to set their quarry and pressure it to move this way and that, all in accordance with the sanctioners' interest and with the intent of the target reaching the exit. Sanctions, after all, are not about catching the enemy or trapping it. As the Japanese after the oil embargo and Saddam Hussein after the first Gulf War showed, a trapped enemy has no options and few ways of satisfying its adversaries to a mutually satisfactory degree. So, such trapped enemies respond—as many do—with their backs against the wall.

Rather, the objective is to design a maze around the sanctioned quarry that drives them to make the policy switch desired by the sanctioner, thereby completing the maze. Walls should be built up to isolate them from less desirable outcomes (e.g., sanctions evasion). Multiple paths to the same, desired end state should be laid out. And, all the while, the quarry should be channeled in the direction the sanctioner determines.

The principal task of the sanctions designer and analyst is to anticipate how the quarry will run, and in which direction; to build a maze that adapts to the quarry running along its halls, ever chivvying it to the desired end. Ensuring that the maze is well designed and serving this function ought to be the preoccupation of the senior leadership of the sanctioning country, who must hold their sanctioners and diplomats responsible for building a maze that works, is well contained, but still gets quarry and sanctioner to the finish. They should be continually thinking about how to close off escape routes and how best to drive their opponent to the outcome they've selected.

Finally, when this outcome is reached, they must let the quarry enjoy the benefits of having completed the maze. The quarry must feel satisfied that it has reached the desired outcome and must believe that, having done what the maze-builder sought all along, they are now free to move about as they wish. They must understand—and all those observing the cat-and-mouse game of our sanctioner and sanctioned parties—that having met the desired end state of the sanctioner, they can have respite from the sanctions and garner the benefits they've been promised. Failing to accept victory and instead defining new ends to the maze is a risk all sanctioners must manage. But if they are prudent, sanctioners will be as able to say "yes" to the outcome of the maze they have designed as the sanctioned parties are willing to go to that outcome, mindful that it is not just the specific sanctions target that is the audience for the sanctions but also the entirety of the international community, members of which may in the future be asked to run a similar maze.

Last, the sanctioning maze builder must be prepared to decide that its subject will be unable to complete the maze on its own and to consider whether help in meeting the desired end state or acceptance of lesser objectives are reasonable outcomes. For it is not just the quarry running the maze that has a latent interest in the end being reached. Sanctioners also want their target to succeed because, only then, will they themselves have used their art to solve the problem set before them. Agility, flexibility, creativity, and adaptability are the core attributes of a sanctioner, at least one that effectively enlists the brute force of the tool to its intended diplomatic purpose.

Notes

Introduction

1. Xie Tao, "How Did China Lose South Korea?," *The Diplomat*, March 9, 2017, http://thediplomat.com/2017/03/how-did-china-lose-south-korea/.

2. Gary Hufbauer, Jeffrey Schott, and Ann Elliott, *Economic Sanctions Reconsidered*, 3rd ed. (Washington, DC: Peterson Institute for International Economics, 2007), appendix 1A.

1. Defining Terms

1. Thomas Schelling, *Arms and Influence* (New Haven, CT: Yale University Press, 1966), v.

2. Ibid., 2.

3. Ibid., 33.

4. Richard Ned Lebow, "Conclusions," in *Psychology and Deterrence*, by Robert Jervis, Richard Ned Lebow, and Janice Gross Stein (Baltimore: Johns Hopkins University Press, 1985), 216.

2. Iraq

1. Mehran Kamrava, *The Modern Middle East: A Political History Since the First World War* (Berkeley: University of California Press, 2005), 185–86.
2. "Transcript of Blix's UN Presentation," *CNN*, March 7, 2003, http://www.cnn.com/2003/US/03/07/sprj.irq.un.transcript.blix/.
3. Central Intelligence Agency, "Comprehensive Report of the Special Advisor to the DCI on Iraq's WMD, Chapter on Regime Strategic Intent," September 30, 2004, https://www.cia.gov/library/reports/general-reports-1/iraq_wmd_2004/chap1.html#sect6.
4. Meghan L. O'Sullivan, *Shrewd Sanctions: State Sponsors of Terrorism* (Washington, DC: Brookings Institution Press, 2003), 123–125.
5. Peter Boone, Haris Gazdar, and Athar Hussein, "Sanctions Against Iraq: Costs of Failure," Report for the Center for Economic and Social Rights, November 1997, http://www.cesr.org/downloads/Sanctions%20Against%20Iraq%20Costs%20of%20Failure%201997.pdf.
6. Transcript of Hearing before the Permanent Subcommittee on Investigations of the Committee on Governmental Affairs of the U.S. Senate, "How Saddam Hussein Abused the United Nations Oil-For-Food Program," November 15, 2004, http://www.gpo.gov/fdsys/pkg/CHRG-108shrg97048/pdf/CHRG-108shrg97048.pdf.
7. United Nations, "Oil For Food," http://www.un.org/Depts/oip/background/, accessed January 10, 2016.

3. Taking on Iran

1. State Department cable from Tehran, May 11, 1977, http://nsarchive.gwu.edu/nukevault/ebb268/doc14b.pdf.
2. Ariana Rowberry, "Sixty Years of Atoms for Peace and Iran's Nuclear Program," *Up Front* (blog), *Brookings*, December 18, 2013, http://www.brookings.edu/blogs/up-front/posts/2013/12/18-sixty-years-atoms-peace-iran-nuclear-program-rowberry.
3. State Department cable from Tehran, May 11, 1977.
4. Andrew Scott Cooper, *The Oil Kings* (New York: Simon and Schuster, 2011).
5. David Albright and Andrea Stricker, "Iran's Nuclear Program," *Iran Primer* (blog), United States Institute of Peace, September 2015, http://iranprimer.usip.org/resource/irans-nuclear-program.

6. IAEA Report to the Board of Governors, "Implementation of the NPT Safeguards Agreement in the Islamic Republic of Iran," November 15, 2014, https://www.iaea.org/sites/default/files/gov2004-83.pdf.

7. Michael Laufer, "A. Q. Khan Nuclear Chronology," *Carnegie Endowment for International Peace*, September 7, 2005, http://carnegieendowment .org/2005/09/07/a.-q.-khan-nuclear-chronology.

8. A CSA provides legal authority for the IAEA to conduct inspections of declared nuclear facilities within a country.

9. Thomas W. Lippman, "U.S. Defers Sanctions on Iran Gas Deal," *Washington Post*, October 4, 1997, https://www.washingtonpost.com /archive/politics/1997/10/04/us-defers-sanctions-on-iran-gas-deal/6f4a72cb -f760-4eaa-9ea6-bdf3c2de52f2/?utm_term=.106afb70c72c

10. IAEA Report to the Board of Governors, "Implementation of the NPT Safeguards Agreement," November 15, 2004, https://www.iaea.org/sites /default/files/gov2004-83.pdf.

11. Ibid.

12. Ibid.

13. IAEA Statute, https://www.iaea.org/about/statute.

14. "Iran Rejects Europe's Nuclear Deal," *CNN*, August 9, 2005, http:// www.cnn.com/2005/WORLD/meast/08/06/iran.nuclear/index.html?; IAEA Report to the Board of Governors, "Implementation of the NPT Safeguards Agreement," September 2, 2005, https://www.iaea.org/sites/default /files/gov2005-67.pdf.

15. IAEA Board of Governors resolution, September 24, 2005, https:// www.iaea.org/sites/default/files/gov2005-77.pdf.

16. Paul Kerr, "IAEA Reports Iran to UN Security Council," *Arms Control Today*, March 1, 2006, https://www.armscontrol.org/act/2006_03 /MARCH-IAEAIran.

17. CQ Transcripts Wire, "President Bush's State of the Union Address," *Washington Post*, January 31, 2006, http://www.washingtonpost.com/wp -dyn/content/article/2006/01/31/AR2006013101468.html; UN Security Council, "Security Council, in Presidential Statement, Underlines Importance of Iran's Re-Establishing Full, Sustained Suspension of Uranium-Enrichment Activities," March 29, 2006, http://www.un.org/press/en/2006/sc8679.doc .htm.

18. The exact list of potential sanctions measures agreed to among the P5+1 has not been released publicly, although many of the measures were subsequently adopted by the UNSC in its four resolutions to impose sanctions against Iran. But the incentives offered have been made public (and are contained in an annex to resolution 1747).

19. Breffni O'Rourke, "Iran: Solana Delivers EU Offer on Nuclear Program," Radio Free Europe / Radio Liberty, June 6, 2006, http://www.rferl.org/content/article/1068944.html.

20. Radio Free Europe / Radio Liberty, "Iran: U.S. Official Outlines Concerns About Nuclear Program," October 23, 2006, http://www.rferl.org/content/article/1072217.html.

21. Executive Order 13382, July 1, 2005, http://www.state.gov/documents/organization/135435.pdf.

22. Robin Wright, "Stuart Levey's War," *New York Times*, October 31, 2008, http://www.nytimes.com/2008/11/02/magazine/02IRAN-t.html.

4. On Sanctions Imposition and Pain

1. "Labor Force Statistics from the Current Population Survey, 2007–2017," Bureau of Labor Statistics, https://data.bls.gov/timeseries/LNS14000000.

2. Heather Long, "The U.S. Is 'Basically at Full Employment,'" *CNN Money*, May 23, 2016, http://money.cnn.com/2016/05/23/news/economy/us-full-employment-williams/.

3. Jed Kolko, "Trump Was Stronger Where the Economy Is Weaker," *FiveThirtyEight*, November 10, 2016, http://fivethirtyeight.com/features/trump-was-stronger-where-the-economy-is-weaker/.

4. Of course, another target of the information war that any sanctions campaign must involve are other states worldwide, either in service of creating a coalition of "likeminded" states that might join a sanctions effort or to ward off any other states that could seek to offer solace to the principle target of the campaign. Sanctioners should be aware of how the target states and the sanctions effort will be perceived—a prudent response to an unacceptable challenge or bullying of the weak by the strong—and how they can use this information element to advance their sanctions goals.

5. Richard Nephew, "Issue Brief: The Future of Economic Sanctions in a Global Economy," Columbia/SIPA Center on Global Energy Policy, May 2015, https://gallery.mailchimp.com/20fec43d5e4f6bc717201530a/files/Issue_Brief_The_Future_of_Economic_Sanctions_in_a_Global_Economy_May_2015.pdf.

6. Stephanie Curcuru and Charles Thomas, "The Return on U.S. Direct Investment at Home and Abroad," *International Finance Discussion Papers* (2012), http://www.federalreserve.gov/pubs/ifdp/2012/1057/ifdp1057.pdf.

7. Pew Research Center, "UN Retains Strong Global Image," September 17, 2013, http://www.pewglobal.org/2013/09/17/united-nations-retains -strong-global-image/.

5. Pressure Begins on Iran

1. U.S. Department of the Treasury, "Fact Sheet: Designation of Iranian Entities and Individuals for Proliferation Activities and Support for Terrorism," October 25, 2007, https://www.treasury.gov/press-center/press-releases /Pages/hp644.aspx.

2. IAEA Report to the Board of Governors, "Implementation of the NPT Safeguards Agreement and Relevant Provisions of Security Council Resolutions 1737 (2006) and 1747 (2007) in the Islamic Republic of Iran," February 22, 2008, https://www.iaea.org/sites/default/files/gov2008-4.pdf.

3. UN Security Council Resolution 1747, Adopted March 24, 2007, https://www.iaea.org/sites/default/files/unsc_res1747-2007.pdf.

4. International Monetary Fund, "Public Information Notice No 08/86: IMF Executive Board Concludes 2008 Article IV Consultation with the Islamic Republic of Iran," July 18, 2008, https://www.imf.org/external/np/sec /pn/2008/pn0886.htm.

5. U.S. Department of the Treasury, "Under Secretary for Terrorism and Financial Intelligence Stuart Levey Testimony," April 1, 2008, https://www .treasury.gov/press-center/press-releases/Pages/hp898.aspx.

6. Bertrand Benoit, "Berlin Hardens Trade Stance with Iran," *Financial Times*, February 11, 2008, https://next.ft.com/content/3c87de5c-d8cc-11dc -8b22-0000779fd2ac.

7. Export Finance and Insurance Corporation, "Escalating Sanctions Are Squeezing Iran's Economy: EFIC," August 4, 2008, http://www.ferret .com.au/c/Export-Finance-and-Insurance-Corporation-EFIC/Escalating -sanctions-are-squeezing-Iran-s-economy-EFIC-n810924.

8. U.S. Department of the Treasury, "Testimony of Stuart Levey, Under Secretary Office of Terrorism and Financial Intelligence," October 6, 2009, http://www.banking.senate.gov/public/_cache/files/ba2f68c0-2484-4797 -adf0-0585253f195b/33A699FF535D59925B69836A6E068FD0 .leveytestimony10609.pdf.

9. Daniel Dombey, "U.S. Imposes Fresh Sanctions on Iran," *Financial Times*, September 11, 2008, http://www.ft.com/cms/s/0/75f9924c-7f99-11dd-a3da -000077b07658.html?ft_site=falcon&desktop=true#axzz4GUN9AwR1.

10. Text of UNSCR 1929, June 10, 2010, http://www.un.org/press/en
/2010/sc9948.doc.htm.

11. Treasury Department Press Release, "Treasury Targets Iranian Arms
Shipments," March 27, 2012.

12. The successor to ILSA, which had the Libya-related prongs removed
following Libya's 2003 decision to give up its WMD programs and support
for terrorism.

6. On Target Response and Resolve

1. Nick Miroff and Karen DeYoung, "New U.S. Sanctions Lost in
Venezuela's Translation," *Washington Post*, March 11, 2015, https://www
.washingtonpost.com/world/the_americas/new-us-sanctions-lost-in-venezuelas
-translation/2015/03/11/f8f3af6a-c7ff-11e4-bea5-b893e7ac3fb3_story.html.

2. AFP, "U.S. Lawmaker Urges Iranian Gasoline Embargo," February 10,
2010, http://www.iranfocus.com/en/index.php?option=com_content&view
=article&id=19770:us-lawmaker-urges-iranian-gasoline-embargo&catid=8
:nuclear&Itemid=113.

3. Official data from the National Iranian Oil Refining and Distribution
Company, courtesy of FGE.

4. Central Intelligence Agency, September 30, 2004, "Comprehensive
Report of the Special Advisor to the DCI on Iraq's WMD," https://www.cia
.gov/library/reports/general-reports-1/iraq_wmd_2004/.

5. Suzanne Maloney, *Iran's Political Economy Since the Revolution* (Cambridge: Cambridge University Press, 2015), 337–338.

6. Ora Coren and Zvi Zrahiya, "Knesset Report: BDS Movement Has
No Impact on Economy," *Haaretz*, January 9, 2015, http://www.haaretz.com
/israel-news/.premium-1.636172; RAND International Center for Middle
East Public Policy, "Calculating the Costs of the Israeli-Palestinian Conflict,"
http://www.rand.org/international/cmepp/costs-of-conflict/calculator.html;
John Reed, "Israel: A New Kind of War," *Financial Times*, June 12, 2015,
http://www.ft.com/intl/cms/s/0/f11c1e1c-0e13-11e5-8ce9-00144feabdc0
.html#axzz3pP9sY2Oy.

7. " 'Netanyahu Failed in Stemming Tide of BDS Against Israel,' Herzog
Says," *JPost.com*, June 5, 2015, http://www.jpost.com/Israel-News/Politics-
And-Diplomacy/Netanyahu-failed-in-stemming-tide-of-BDS-against-Israel
-Herzog-says-405166.

8. IAEA Reports to the Board of Governors, "Implementation of the NPT Safeguards Agreement and Relevant Provisions of Security Council Resolutions in the Islamic Republic of Iran," August 2009 and February 2011, https://www .iaea.org/newscenter/focus/iran/iaea-and-iran-iaea-reports.

9. "Saddam 'Wins 100% of Vote,'" *BBC News*, October 16, 2002, http:// news.bbc.co.uk/2/hi/2331951.stm.

10. Terror Free Tomorrow, "Polling Iranian Public Opinion: An Unprecedented Nation-wide Survey of Iran," June 5, 2007, http://www.terrorfree tomorrow.org/upimagestft/TFT%20Iran%20Survey%20Report.pdf.

11. Sara Beth Elson and Alireza Nader, "What Do Iranians Think?" RAND Corporation, 2011, http://www.rand.org/pubs/technical_reports/TR910 .html.

12. Nancy Gallagher, Ebrahim Mohseni, and Clay Ramsay, "Iranian Public Opinion on the Nuclear Negotiations," Center for International and Security Studies, University of Maryland, June 2015, http://www.cissm.umd .edu/publications/iranian-public-opinion-nuclear-negotiations.

7. Intense Pressure on Iran and a Turn to Real Negotiations

1. Jeffrey Goldberg, "Obama to Iran and Israel: 'As President of the United States, I Don't Bluff,'" *Atlantic*, March 2, 2012, https://www.theatlantic.com /international/archive/2012/03/obama-to-iran-and-israel-as-president-of -the-united-states-i-dont-bluff/253875/.

2. "Examining OFAC Guidance on NDAA Iran Sanctions," *Law360*, March 5, 2012, https://www.law360.com/articles/316088/examining-ofac-guidance -on-ndaa-iran-sanctions.

3. "Iran's Economy, By the Numbers," *Iran Primer* (blog), United States Institute of Peace, May 11, 2015, http://iranprimer.usip.org/blog/2015/may/11 /irans-economy-numbers.

4. Matt O'Brien, "How Does a Currency Drop 60 Percent in 8 Days? Just Ask Iran," *Atlantic*, October 2, 2012, http://www.theatlantic.com/business/archive /2012/10/how-does-a-currency-drop-60-in-8-days-just-ask-iran/263159/.

5. Meir Javedanfar, "Iran's Big Crisis: The Price of Chicken," *Bloomberg*, August 7, 2012, http://www.bloombergview.com/articles/2012-08-07/iran -s-big-crisis-the-price-of-chicken.

6. BBC Persia, (in Persian), March 2007, http://www.bbc.com/persian /business/story/2007/03/070303_mv-five-thousand.shtml.

7. Terror Free Tomorrow, "Polling Iranian Public Opinion: An Unprecedented Nationwide Survey of Iran" (2007), http://www.terrorfreetomorrow .org/upimagestft/TFT%20Iran%20Survey%20Report.pdf.

8. Nancy Gallagher, Ebrahim Mohseni, and Clay Ramsay, "Iranian Public Opinion on the Nuclear Agreement," Center for International and Security Studies, University of Maryland, September 2015, http://www.cissm.umd.edu /publications/iranian-public-opinion-nuclear-agreement.

9. Suzanne Maloney, "Iran's Economy in the Shadow of Regional Upheaval," *Iran Primer* (blog), United States Institute of Peace, February 28, 2011, http://iranprimer.usip.org/blog/2011/feb/28/iran%E2%80%99s-economy -shadow-regional-upheaval.

10. International Monetary Fund (IMF), "Islamic Republic of Iran: 2011 Article IV Consultation Staff Report," August 3, 2011, https://www.imf.org /external/pubs/cat/longres.aspx?sk=25133.0.

11. IAEA Report to the Board of Governors, "Final Assessment on Past and Present Outstanding Issues Regarding the Iranian Nuclear Programme," December 2, 2015, https://www.iaea.org/newscenter/focus /iran/iaea-and-iran-iaea-reports; Director of National Intelligence, "Iran: Nuclear Intentions and Capabilities," December 3, 2007, https:// www.dni.gov/files/documents/Newsroom/Reports%20and%20Pubs /20071203_release.pdf.

8. On the Search for Inflection Points

1. Richard Nephew, "Issue Brief: The Future of Economic Sanctions in a Global Economy," May 2015, https://gallery.mailchimp.com/20fec43d5e 4f6bc717201530a/files/Issue_Brief_The_Future_of_Economic_Sanctions _in_a_Global_Economy_May_2015.pdf.

2. Daniel Yergin, *The Quest* (New York: Penguin, 2012), 233.

3. International Campaign for Human Rights in Iran, *A Growing Crisis: The Impact of Sanctions and Regime Policies on Iranians' Economic and Social Rights* (2013), 143–51, https://www.iranhumanrights.org/wp-content /uploads/A-Growing-Crisis.pdf.

4. Yeganeh Torbati, Bozorgmehr Sharafedin, and Babak Dehghanpisheh, "After Iran's Nuclear Pact, State Firms Win Most Foreign Deals," *Reuters*, January 19, 2017, http://www.reuters.com/article/us-iran-contracts-insight -idUSKBN15328S.

9. Looking Ahead

1. 2015 National Security Strategy of the United States, February 1, 2015, https://www.whitehouse.gov/sites/default/files/docs/2015_national _security_strategy.pdf.

2. Reuters, "Senior Saudi Prince Says Trump Shouldn't Scrap Iran Deal," November 11, 2016, http://www.reuters.com/article/us-usa-election-saudi -iran-idUSKBN1361SS.

3. Richard Nephew, "Sanctions Relief Won't Be a $100 Billion Windfall for Iran's Terrorist Friends," *Foreign Policy*, July 2, 2015, http://foreignpolicy.com /2015/07/02/iran-rouhani-khamenei-syria-assad-nuclear-sanctions-hezbollah/.

4. Bradley Hope, "U.K.'s Iranian-Owned Banks, Freed of Sanctions, Now Face Trust Barriers," *Wall Street Journal*, March 8, 2017, https:// www.wsj.com/articles/u-k-s-iranian-owned-banks-freed-of-sanctions-now -face-trust-barriers-1488978001.

5. Golnar Motevalli, "Top Banks in Iran Dragged into Rouhani Tussle with Rivals," *Bloomberg*, September 5, 2016, https://www.bloomberg.com /news/articles/2016-09-05/top-iran-banks-dragged-into-rouhani-tussle-with -hardline-rivals.

6. Derek Frazer, "The Refusal of President Yanukovych of Ukraine to Sign at the EU Vilnius Summit on 28 to 29 November the Association Agreement Including a Deep and Comprehensive Free Trade Area (DCFTA) with the European Union," EUCAnet.org, December 3, 2013, http://www.eucanet.org /news/media-tips/6-international-relations/169-the-refusal-of-president -yanukovych-of-ukraine-to-sign-at-the-eu-vilnius-summit-on-28-to-29 -november-the-association-agreement-including-a-deep-and-comprehensive -free-trade-area-dcfta-with-the-european-union; David Herszenhorn, "Russia Putting a Strong Arm on Neighbors," *New York Times*, October 22, 2013, http://www.nytimes.com/2013/10/23/world/europe/russia-putting-a-strong -arm-on-neighbors.html.

7. "Ukraine Crisis: Timeline," *BBC News*, http://www.bbc.com/news/world -middle-east-26248275.

8. Richard Nephew, "Issue Brief: Revisiting Oil Sanctions on Russia," Columbia/SIPA Center on Global Energy Policy, July 2015, http://energypolicy .columbia.edu/sites/default/files/energy/Issue%20Brief_Revisiting%20Oil %20Sanctions%20on%20Russia_Nephew_July%202015.pdf.

9. Energy Information Agency, Database of Oil Prices, http://www.eia .gov/dnav/pet/PET_PRI_SPT_S1_D.htm.

10. Aditya Tejas, "Putin Says Sanctions Amid Falling Oil Prices Cost Russia $160B, But Economy Will Recover," *IBTimes*, April 28, 2015, http://www.ibtimes.com/putin-says-sanctionsamid-falling-oil-prices-cost-russia-160b-economywill-recover-1899194; International Monetary Fund (IMF), "Russian Federation: 2014 Article IV Consultation Staff Report," http://www.imf.org/external/pubs/ft/scr/2014/ cr14175.pdf.

11. Nephew, "Issue Brief: Revisiting Oil Sanctions on Russia."

12. Evgenia Pismennaya, "Putin's Bailout Bank Needs a Rescue; It's a $18 Billion Whopper," *Bloomberg*, December 28, 2015, http://www.bloomberg.com/news/articles/2015-12-28/putin-s-bailout-bank-needs-a-rescue-it-s-an-18-billion-whopper.

13. Vladimir Kuznetsov, "Ruble Drops to 2015 Low on Year-End Budget Flows as Oil Tumbles," *Bloomberg*, December 28, 2015, http://www.bloomberg.com/news/articles/2015-12-28/ruble-drops-to-2015-low-on-year-end-budget-flows-as-oil-tumbles.

14. White House Press Office, "Statement by the President on Ukraine," March 20, 2014, https://www.whitehouse.gov/the-press-office/2014/03/20/statement-president-ukraine.

15. Kenneth Rapoza, "One Year After Russia Annexed Crimea, Locals Prefer Moscow to Kiev," *Forbes*, March 20, 2015, http://www.forbes.com/sites/kenrapoza/2015/03/20/one-year-after-russia-annexed-crimea-locals-prefer-moscow-to-kiev/.

16. "Minsk Agreement on Ukraine Crisis: Text in Full," *Telegraph*, February 12, 2015, http://www.telegraph.co.uk/news/worldnews/europe/ukraine/11408266/Minsk-agreement-on-Ukraine-crisis-text-in-full.html.

17. Levada Center website, homepage. Accessed on January 6, 2016. http://www.levada.ru/eng/.

18. Jonathan Wheatley, "Russia to Issue Renminbi Denominated Debt," *Financial Times*, December 7, 2015, http://www.ft.com/cms/s/3/6b7036c4-9a8e-11e5-a5c1-ca5db4add713.html#axzz3vpvUdMgC.

19. James Paton and Aibing Guo, "Russia, China Add to $400 Billion Gas Deal with Accord," *Bloomberg*, November 9, 2014, http://www.bloomberg.com/news/articles/2014-11-10/russia-china-add-to-400-billion-gas-deal-with-accord.

20. Robert S. Boynton, "North Korea's Abduction Program," *New Yorker*, December 21, 2015, http://www.newyorker.com/news/news-desk/north-koreas-abduction-project.

21. Julian Ryall, "South Korea Investigates Reports of 'Invasion Tunnels' from North," *Telegraph*, October 28, 2014, http://www.telegraph.co.uk/news/worldnews/asia/northkorea/11192736/South-Korea-investigates-reports-of-invasion-tunnels-from-North.html.

22. Colin Schulz, "The Time the U.S. Nearly Nuked North Korea over a Highjacked Spy Ship," *Smithsonian*, January 28, 2014, http://www .smithsonianmag.com/smart-news/time-us-nearly-nuked-north-korea-over -highjacked-spy-ship-180949514/.

23. UN Secretariat, "The List Established and Maintained Pursuant to Security Council res. 1718 (2006)," https://scsanctions.un.org/fop/fop?xml =htdocs/resources/xml/en/consolidated.xml&xslt=htdocs/resources/xsl/en /dprk.xsl.

24. Ministry of Foreign Affairs of Japan, "Measures taken by the Government of Japan against North Korea," December 2, 2016, http://www.mofa .go.jp/a_o/na/kp/page3e_000628.html.

25. Benjamin Lee, "THAAD and the Sino-South Korean Strategic Dilemma," *The Diplomat* (October 2016), http://thediplomat.com/2016/10 /thaad-and-the-sino-south-korean-strategic-dilemma/.

26. Julian Ryall, "North Korea Losing African, South American Allies," *Deutsche Welle*, June 21, 2016, http://www.dw.com/en/north-korea-losing -african-south-american-allies/a-19344851.

27. Kelsey Davenport, "Chronology of U.S.-North Korean Nuclear and Missile Diplomacy," Arms Control Association, March 2017, https://www .armscontrol.org/factsheets/dprkchron.

28. Jonathan Watts, "China Cuts Oil Supply to North Korea, *Guardian*, March 31, 2003, https://www.theguardian.com/world/2003/apr/01/northkorea .china; Scott Conroy, "North Korea to Rejoin Six Party Talks," *CBS News*, October 31, 2006, http://www.cbsnews.com/news/north-korea-to-rejoin-six -party-talks//.

29. Aaron Stein, "North Korea Tested an H Bomb?," *Arms Control Wonk*, January 6, 2016, http://www.armscontrolwonk.com/archive/1200732/north -korea-tested-an-h-bomb/.

30. Jeffrey Lewis, "North Korea's Nuke Program Is Way More Sophisticated Than You Think," *Foreign Policy*, September 9, 2016, http://foreignpolicy. com/2016/09/09/north-koreas-nuclear-program-is-way-more-sophisticated -and-dangerous-than-you-think/.

31. Josh Rogin, "Inside the Secret U.S.-North Korea 'Track 2' Diplomacy," *Washington Post*, August 28, 2016, https://www.washingtonpost.com /opinions/global-opinions/inside-the-secret-us-north-korea-track-2 -diplomacy/2016/08/28/ef33b2d4-6bc0-11e6-ba32-5a4bf5aad4fa_story. html?utm_term=.6f37f529c80b.

32. Joint Statement of the Fourth Round of the Six Party Talks, September 19, 2005, https://www.state.gov/p/eap/regional/c15455.htm.

33. Ibid.

34. Georgy Toloraya, "Deciphering North Korean Economic Policy Intentions," *38 North*, July 26, 2016, http://38north.org/2016/07/gtoloraya 072616/.

Conclusion

1. William H. Overholt, *Political Risk* (London: Euromoney, 1982), 3.

Bibliography

AFP. "U.S. Lawmaker Urges Iranian Gasoline Embargo." February 19, 2010. http://www.iranfocus.com/en/index.php?option=com_content&view=article&id=19770:us-lawmaker-urges-iranian-gasoline-embargo&catid=8:nuclear&Itemid=113.

Albright, David, and Andrea Stricker. "Iran's Nuclear Program." *Iran Primer* (blog), United States Institute of Peace. September 2015. http://iranprimer.usip.org/resource/irans-nuclear-program.

Allen, Susan. "The Domestic Political Costs of Economic Sanctions." *Journal of Conflict Resolution* 52, no. 6 (2008): 916–44.

Andreas, Peter. "Criminalizing Consequences of Sanctions: Embargo Busting and Its Legacy." *International Studies Quarterly* 49, no. 2 (2005): 335–60.

Askari, Hossein G., John Forrer, Hildy Teegan, and Jiawen Yang. *Economic Sanctions: Examining their Philosophy and Efficacy*. Westport, Conn.: Praeger, 2003.

Baldwin, David. *Economic Statecraft*. Princeton: Princeton University Press, 1985.

Baldwin, David and Robert Pape. "Evaluating Economic Sanctions." *International Security* 23, no. 2 (Fall 1998): 189–98.

BBC.com. "Ukraine Crisis: Timeline." Accessed January 2010. http://www.bbc.com/news/world-middle-east-26248275.

Bolks, Sean, and Dina al-Sowayel. "How Long Do Economic Sanctions Last? Examining the Sanctioning Process Through Duration." *Political Research Quarterly* 53, no. 2 (2000): 241–65.

Boone, Peter, Haris Gazdar, and Athar Hussein. "Sanctions Against Iraq: Costs of Failure." Report for the Center for Economic and Social Rights (November 1997). http://www.cesr.org/downloads/Sanctions%20Against%20Iraq%20Costs%20of%20Failure%201997.pdf.

Central Intelligence Agency. "Comprehensive Report of the Special Advisor to the DCI on Iraq's WMD, Chapter on Regime Strategic Intent" (September 30, 2004). https://www.cia.gov/library/reports/general-reports-1/iraq_wmd_2004/chap1.html#sect6.

CNN.com. "Transcript of Blix's UN Presentation." March 7, 2003. http://www.cnn.com/2003/US/03/07/sprj.irq.un.transcript.blix/.

Cooper, Andrew Scott. *The Oil Kings.* New York: Simon and Schuster, 2011.

Copeland, Cassandra, Curtis Jolly, and Henry Thompson. "The History and Potential Trade Between Cuba and the United States." *Journal of Business and Economics* 2, no. 3 (2011): 163–74. http://www.auburn.edu/~thomph1/cubahistory.pdf.

Coren, Ora, and Zvi Zrahiya. "Knesset Report: BDS Movement Has No Impact on Economy." *Haaretz*, January 9, 2015. http://www.haaretz.com/israel-news/.premium-1.636172.

Cortright, David, and George Lopez, eds. *The Sanctions Decade: Assessing UN Strategies in the 1990s.* Boulder, Colo.: Lynne Reiner, 2000.

Curcuru, Stephanie, and Charles Thomas. "The Return on US Direct Investment at Home and Abroad." *International Finance Discussion Papers* (2012). http://www.federalreserve.gov/pubs/ifdp/2012/1057/ifdp1057.pdf.

Drezner, Daniel. *The Sanctions Paradox: Economic Statecraft and International Relations.* Cambridge: Cambridge University Press, 1999.

Energy Information Agency. Database of Oil Prices. http://www.eia.gov/dnav/pet/PET_PRI_SPT_S1_D.htm

Escriba-Folch, Abel, and Joseph Wright. "Dealing with Tyranny: International Sanctions and the Survival of Authoritarian Rulers." *International Studies Quarterly* 54, no. 2 (2010): 335–59.

Facts, Global, Energy (FGE) email from on December 10, 2015, relaying official data from the National Iranian Oil Refining and Distribution Company.

Frazer, Derek. "The Refusal of President Yanukovych of Ukraine to Sign at the EU Vilnius Summit on 28 to 29 November, the Association Agreement, Including a Deep and Comprehensive Free Trade Area (DCFTA) with the European Union" (December 3, 2013). http://www.eucanet.org/news/media-tips/6-international-relations/169-the-refusal-of-president-yanukovych-of-ukraine-to-sign-at-the-eu-vilnius-summit-on-28-to-29-november-the-association-agreement-including-a-deep-and-comprehensive-free-trade-area-dcfta-with-the-european-union.

Gallagher, Nancy, Ebrahim Mohseni, and Clay Ramsay. "Iranian Public Opinion on the Nuclear Agreement" (September 2015). http://www.cissm .umd.edu/publications/iranian-public-opinion-nuclear-agreement.

George, Alexander. *Forceful Persuasion: Coercive Diplomacy as an Alternative to War.* Washington, DC: U.S. Institute for Peace, 1991.

Haass, Richard. *Economic Sanctions and American Diplomacy.* New York: Council on Foreign Relations Press, 1998.

Haass, Richard, and Meghan O'Sullivan. *Honey and Vinegar: Incentives, Sanctions, and Foreign Policy.* Washington, DC: Brookings, 2000.

Herszenhorn, David. "Russia Putting a Strong Arm on Neighbors." *New York Times,* October 22, 2013. http://www.nytimes.com/2013/10/23/world /europe/russia-putting-a-strong-arm-on-neighbors.html.

Hufbauer, Gary, Jeffrey Schott, and Ann Elliott. *Economic Sanctions Reconsidered,* 3rd ed. Washington, DC: Peterson Institute for International Economics, 2007.

IAEA Report to the Board of Governors. "Final Assessment on Past and Present Outstanding Issues Regarding the Iranian Nuclear Programme" (December 2, 2015). https://www.iaea.org/newscenter/focus/iran/iaea-and -iran-iaea-reports.

IAEA Report to the Board of Governors. "Implementation of the NPT Safeguards Agreement and Relevant Provisions of Security Council resolutions in the Islamic Republic of Iran" (August 2009, February 2011, and November 2011). https://www.iaea.org/newscenter/focus/iran/iaea-and -iran-iaea-reports.

International Campaign for Human Rights in Iran. *A Growing Crisis: The Impact of Sanctions and Regime Policies on Iranians' Economic and Social Rights.* New York: International Campaign for Human Rights in Iran, 2013.

International Monetary Fund (IMF). "Islamic Republic of Iran: 2011 Article IV Consultation Staff Report" (August 3, 2011). https://www.imf.org/external /pubs/cat/longres.aspx?sk=25133.0.

Iran Primer (blog), United States Institute of Peace. "Iran's Economy, By the Numbers." May 11, 2015. http://iranprimer.usip.org/blog/2015/may/11/irans -economy-numbers.

——. "Russian Federation: 2014 Article IV Consultation Staff Report" (July 2014). http://www.imf.org/external/pubs/ft/scr/2014/ cr14175.pdf.

Javendanfar, Meir. "Iran's Big Crisis: The Price of Chicken." *Bloomberg,* August 7, 2012. http://www.bloombergview.com/articles/2012-08-07 /iran-s-big-crisis-the-price-of-chicken.

Jordan, Will, and Rahul Radhakrishnan. "Mossad Contradicted Netanyahu on Iran Nuclear Programme." *Al Jazeera,* February 23, 2015. http://www

.aljazeera.com/news/2015/02/leaks-netanyahu-misled-iran-nuclear-programme-guardian-iran-nuclear-speech-2012-150218165622065.html.

JPost.com. "'Netanyahu Failed in Stemming Tide of BDS Against Israel,' Herzog Says." June 5, 2015. http://www.jpost.com/Israel-News/Politics -And-Diplomacy/Netanyahu-failed-in-stemming-tide-of-BDS-against -Israel-Herzog-says-405166.

Kaempfer, William, Anton Lowenberg, and William Mertens. "International Economic Sanctions Against a Dictator." *Economics and Politics* 16, no. 1 (March 2004): 29–51.

Kamrava, Mehran. *The Modern Middle East: A Political History Since the First World War.* Berkeley: University of California Press, 2005.

Keynes, John Maynard. *The Economic Consequences of Peace.* New York: Harcourt, Brace, and Howe, 1919.

Kuznetsov, Vladimir. "Ruble Drops to 2015 Low on Year-End Budget Flows as Oil Tumbles." *Bloomberg,* December 28, 2015. http://www.bloomberg .com/news/articles/2015-12-28/ruble-drops-to-2015-low-on-year-end -budget-flows-as-oil-tumbles.

Lebow, Ned. "The Deterrence Deadlock: Is There a Way Out?" and "Conclusions" in *Psychology and Deterrence*, ed. Robert Jervis, et al., 180–232. Baltimore: Johns Hopkins University Press, 1985.

Levada Center website, homepage, http://www.levada.ru/eng/.

Licht, Amanda. "Falling Out of Favor: Economic Sanctions and the Tenure of Leaders" (2011). Visions in Methodology. http://visionsinmethodology .org/wp-content/uploads/2011/09/LichtMPSA2011FallingOutOfFavor.pdf.

Maloney, Suzanne. *Iran's Political Economy Since the Revolution.* Cambridge: Cambridge University Press, 2015.

Marshall, George. "Speech at Harvard University, 5 June 1947." http://www .oecd.org/general/themarshallplanspeechatharvarduniversity5june1947.htm.

Martin, Lisa. *Coercive Cooperation.* Princeton: Princeton University Press, 1992.

Miroff, Nick, and Karen DeYoung. "New U.S. Sanctions Lost in Venezuela's Translation." *Washington Post,* March 11, 2015. https://www.washington post.com/world/the_americas/new-us-sanctions-lost-in-venezuelas -translation/2015/03/11/f8f3af6a-c7ff-11e4-bea5-b893e7ac3fb3_story.html.

Nephew, Richard. "Issue Brief: Revisiting Oil Sanctions on Russia." Columbia/SIPA Center on Global Energy Policy, July 2015. http://energypolicy. columbia.edu/sites/default/files/energy/Issue%20Brief_Revisiting%20 Oil%20Sanctions%20on%20Russia_Nephew_July%202015.pdf.

——. "Issue Brief: The Future of Economic Sanctions in a Global Economy" Columbia/SIPA Center on Global Energy Policy, May 2015. https://gallery

.mailchimp.com/20fec43d5e4f6bc717201530a/files/Issue_Brief_The _Future_of_Economic_Sanctions_in_a_Global_Economy_May_2015.pdf.

——. "Sanctions Relief Won't Be a $100 Billion Windfall for Iran's Terrorist Friends." *Foreign Policy*, July 2, 2015. http://foreignpolicy.com/2015/07/02 /iran-rouhani-khamenei-syria-assad-nuclear-sanctions-hezbollah/.

O'Sullivan, Meghan. *Shrewd Sanctions: Statecraft and State Sponsors of Terrorism*. Washington, DC: Brookings, 2003.

Overholt, William H. *Political Risk*. London: Euromoney Publications, 1982.

Pape, Robert. "Why Economic Sanctions Do Not Work." *International Security* 22, no. 2 (1997): 90–136.

Paton, James, and Aibing Guo. "Russia, China Add to $400 Billion Gas Deal with Accord." *Bloomberg*, November 9, 2014. http://www.bloomberg .com/news/articles/2014-11-10/russia-china-add-to-400-billion-gas-deal -with-accord.

Pew Research Center. "UN Retains Strong Global Image." September 17, 2013. http://www.pewglobal.org/2013/09/17/united-nations-retains-strong -global-image/?beta=true&utm_expid=53098246-2.Lly4CFSVQG2lphsg -KopIg.1&utm_referrer=https%3A%2F%2Fwww.google.com%2F.

Pismennaya, Evgenia. "Putin's Bailout Bank Needs a Rescue; It's a $18 Billion Whopper." *Bloomberg*, December 28, 2015. http://www.bloomberg.com /news/articles/2015-12-28/putin-s-bailout-bank-needs-a-rescue-it-s-an -18-billion-whopper.

RAND International Center for Middle East Public Policy. "Calculating the Costs of the Israeli-Palestinian Conflict." http://www.rand.org/international /cmepp/costs-of-conflict/calculator.html.

Rapoza, Kenneth. "One Year After Russia Annexed Crimea, Locals Prefer Moscow to Kiev." *Forbes*, March 20, 2015. http://www.forbes.com/sites /kenrapoza/2015/03/20/one-year-after-russia-annexed-crimea-locals-prefer -moscow-to-kiev/.

Reed, John. "Israel: A New Kind of War." *Financial Times*, June 12, 2015. http://www.ft.com/intl/cms/s/0/f11c1e1c-0e13-11e5-8ce9-00144feabdc0 .html#axzz3pP9sY2Oy.

Rowberry, Ariana. "Sixty Years of Atoms for Peace and Iran's Nuclear Program," *Up Front* (blog), *Brookings*, December 18, 2013. http://www .brookings.edu/blogs/up-front/posts/2013/12/18-sixty-years-atoms -peace-iran-nuclear-program-rowberry.

Rowe, David. "Economic Sanctions Do Work: Economic Statecraft and the Oil Embargo of Rhodesia." In *Power and the Purse: Economic Statecraft, Interdependence, and National Security*, ed. Jean-Marc Blanchard, Edward Mansfield, and Norrin Ripsman, 254–88. New York: Frank Cass, 2000.

Schelling, Thomas. *Arms and Influence*. New Haven: Yale University Press, 1966.

Schultz, Kenneth. *Democracy and Coercive Diplomacy*. Cambridge: Cambridge University Press, 2004.

State Department cable from Tehran, May 11, 1977. http://nsarchive.gwu .edu/nukevault/ebb268/doc14b.pdf.

Taylor, Brendan. *Sanctions as Grand Strategy*. Oxon: Routledge, 2010.

Tejas, Aditya. "Putin Says Sanctions Amid Falling Oil Prices Cost Russia $160B, But Economy Will Recover." *International Business Times*, April 28, 2015. http://www.ibtimes.com/putin-says-sanctionsamid-falling-oil -prices-cost-russia-160b-economywill-recover-1899194.

Terror Free Tomorrow. "Polling Iranian Public Opinion: An Unprecedented Nationwide Survey of Iran" (2007). http://www.terrorfreetomorrow.org /upimagestft/TFT%20Iran%20Survey%20Report.pdf.

Text of the Minsk Two Cease-Fire. http://www.telegraph.co.uk/news /worldnews/europe/ukraine/11408266/Minsk-agreement-on-Ukraine -crisis-text-in-full.html.

Transcript of Hearing Before the Permanent Subcommittee on Investigations of the Committee on Governmental Affairs of the U.S. Senate. "How Saddam Hussein Abused the United Nations Oil-For-Food Program." November 15, 2004. http://www.gpo.gov/fdsys/pkg/CHRG-108 shrg97048/pdf/CHRG-108shrg97048.pdf.

UN "Oil For Food" website, http://www.un.org/Depts/oip/background/.

van Bergeijk, Peter, and Charles van Marrewijk. "Why Do Sanctions Need Time to Work? Adjustment, Learning and Anticipation." *Economic Modeling* 12, no. 2 (1995): 75–86.

Wheatley, Jonathan. "Russia to Issue Renminbi Denominated Debt." *Financial Times*, December 7, 2015. http://www.ft.com/cms/s/3/6b7036c4-9a8e -11e5-a5c1-ca5db4add713.html#axzz3vpvUdMgC.

White House Press Office. "Statement by the President on Ukraine." March 20, 2014. https://www.whitehouse.gov/the-press-office/2014/03/20/statement -president-ukraine.

Woo, Byungwon, and Daniel Verdier. "Sanctions, Rewards and Regime Types." https://polisci.osu.edu/sites/polisci.osu.edu/files/Sanctions,%20rewards %20and%20regime%20type.pdf.

Yergin, Daniel. *The Quest*. New York: Penguin, 2012.

Zarate, Juan. *Treasury's War: The Unleashing of a New Era of Financial Warfare*. New York: PublicAffairs, 2015.

Index

sanctions (*continued*)
relation to, 180; research on,
ix; resistance to, ix–x, 85–87, 103;
response to, 13, 79; sanctioners
implementation of, 14; study of,
23; success or failure of, viii, 4–5,
15, 16; targeted, 142–43, 150–51;
2015 National Security Strategy
mention of, 144–45; violations of,
7–8. *See also* Iran; Iran, pressure
on; Iran, resolve of; Iraq, sanctions
against; Russia; United States
sanctions, against U.S., 61
sanctions, definitions of: confusion
about, 7; as scope of measures, 9;
travel bans, 8–9, 58; workable, 7
sanctions, imposition of, 8, 13,
114; hardship created by, 9;
humanitarian consequences with,
9–12; pain created by, 9–10, 43;
social dynamics of, 15
sanctions, in foreign policy, vii, 8;
attributes of, 3, 4; framework for,
4, 124–25; problems with, 15–16;
of Russia, 2; as tool, 15; of U.S., 2
sanctions, technological: against Iran,
46; against North Korea, 46;
objective of, 45–46; against
Russia, 46
sanctions, types of: diplomatic/
political, 44–45; economic, 46–48;
military, 45; technological, 45–46
sanctions campaign, vii, 32–39, 41
sanctions construction questions:
assessment-based approach to,
59; about economic or political
value, 58, 60; about enforcement,
58; about impact, 58–62; about
physical geography, 58; about
vulnerabilities, 62
sanctions design, vii, ix–x, 3, 60,
62, 162
sanctions failure: confused objectives
as, 133–41; over-reach and

unintended consequences as,
128–33; under-reach as, 126–28
sanctions fatigue, 14
sanctions-focused strategy, 16, 83
sanctions framework, 4; diplomatic
solution conversation in, 182;
identify objectives in, 124, 180–81;
Iran's, 147–55; national priorities
clarity in, 181; North Korea's,
172–78; pain imposition degree in,
181–82; resolve elements in, 182;
Russia's, 161–67; sanctioning state
failure acknowledgment in, 125,
183; scenario of, 125–26; strategy
monitoring in, 125, 182; target
state clear statement of conditions
in, 125, 182; underlying policy
failure in, 183; understand nature
of target in, 125, 181; victory
defining in, 180–81; vulnerabilities
strategy development in, 125,
181–82
Sanctions Paradox, The (Drezner), viii
sanctions response, 13, 79; acceptance
as, 84–85; adaptation as, 85;
Iran's, on gasoline imports, 86–87;
rejection and resistance as, 85–87;
retaliatory sanctions as, 85–86;
Venezuelan example of, 85
Schelling, Thomas, 10
Schengen Zone, 80
Schott, Jeffrey, viii, 125
SDN. *See* Specially Designated
Nationals and Blocked Persons
Section 1245, FY2012 National
Defense Authorization Act, 108
Shah of Iran, 27–29
"Six Party Talks," 170, 172
social dynamics, of sanctions, 15
Solana, Javier, 40
South Korea, 2, 71, 76, 172; China
economic and political ties
improvement seeking of, 169;
North Korea sanctions of, 169;

United States (U.S.) (*continued*)
multinational action development
of, 104; personal communications
technology selling of, 113; Russia
continued pressure by, 160, 162;
Russia expansion of sanctions by,
158–59; Russia sanctions of,
156–57; sanctions, in foreign
policy, 2; sanctions against, 61;
sanctions effort on Iran nuclear
calculus of, 107; shuttle diplomacy
of, 105; Straits of Hormuz tension
between Iran and, 105; Tidewater
Middle East Company sanction
of, 106; TRR project proposal of,
72–73; unintended consequences
of, 130; upper hand in Iran
economy of, 119
UN Monitoring, Verification,
and Inspection Commission
(UNMOVIC), 21
UN Security Council (UNSC):
charter violations of, 18, 20;
General Assembly of, 37; Iran
sanctions with, 40, 189n18; Iran
violations reported to, 39; Israel
and, 62; military sanctions of,
45; North Korea POE's report of,
176; partner sanctions of, 76–77;
resolution 661 of, 18; resolution
687 of, 19; resolution 1718 of,
168–69; resolution 1737 of, 41,
49, 65, 117; resolution 1747 of,
66, 67; resolution 1803 of, 68,

69, 71; resolution 1835 of, 71;
resolution 1929 of, 71, 74, 76, 78;
veto-holding powers of, 40
uranium centrifuge plant, in Iran, 32
uranium conversion facility, of Iran,
38, 41
URENCO, 29
U.S. *See* United States
U.S. embargo, of Iran, 30–31

veto-holding powers, of UNSC, 40
violations, of sanctions, 7–8
vulnerability, 62, 125, 149, 161–62,
173–74, 181–82

War by Other Means (Blackwill and
Harris), viii
weapons of mass destruction (WMD),
64, 192n12; explanation of, 22;
Hussein and, 18, 20–22, 25;
international inspectors for, 23, 34;
in Iran, 32, 33; in Iraq, 18, 20–22,
23, 25, 42
weapons-usable plutonium, in Iran, 32
"Why Economic Sanctions Don't
Work" (Pape), viii
WMD. *See* weapons of mass
destruction
World Bank, 67, 90
World Trade Organization, 31

Yanukovych, Viktor, 157–58

Zarate, Juan, viii, 170